Herding Cats
The Chaotic, Exhausting, & Hilarious Task of Parenting Toddlers

WHITNEY BAUSMAN

DEDICATION

To Clark and Annie. My beautiful, wonderful, uniquely-you 'cats'.

CONTENTS

ACKNOWLEDGMENTS

Jonathan. Your steadfast love and encouragement are the wind in my sails. May our love always be one that is equal parts constant and crazy.

Sue. Without you, my thoughts would be jumbled, misspelled, and unpublished. Thank you for being such an essential part of what I do.

Mom. Never before have I seen you so clearly. Thank you for being the mother you were and are.

Alicia. You make having a half-dozen children look breezy, and you remain my voice of reason and always-protective big sis.

Ashley. Thank you for caring for my babies so well before I was able to claim motherhood as a full-time profession. You know their quirks and their nonstop intensity, but you also know their affection and their humor.

Pastor Steve. Thank you for giving the phrase 'herding cats' residence in my brain. There is no better way to describe my current-day life.

Cassie. Thank you for helping me to believe that the heart of a parent always has room to stretch and grow.

Tristan. Thank you for illustrating the stereotypes of toddlerhood oh-so-well. You will always be one of my favorite little humans.

To the moms in my life who get me and support me best: Kelly, Stacy, Sabrina, Katie, and Kara. In direct and indirect ways, thank you for being a part of these pages.

To my 'tantrum tribe'. Angie, Erin, Laura, Natasha, Amy, Kait, Josh, Bethany, Matt, Emily, April, Kirsten, Rebecca, Colley, Jamy, Stacey, Robin, Suzi, Sharon, Courtney, Andrea, LeeAnn, and Sue. Thank you for contributing to the content of this book in hysterical ways.

And…to the family and friends who boast about me even when I am anything but worthy: Mom, Dad, Tara, Justin, Savanna, and Meg. Thanks!

PROLOGUE: CRAZY CAT LADY REDEFINED

I'm a crazy cat lady, yet I own exactly <u>zero</u> cats. If this isn't computing, allow me to tell you a story...

In the not so distant past, 'herding cats' was an idiom unbeknownst to me. I'd never heard it, and I'd never really experienced it. About six years ago, however, I traveled with a group of folks to a remote village in Ethiopia where I served in a medical clinic. Our team totaled 30-ish members, and it was diverse in both age and vocation. The youngest member of our crew was barely 20 while the eldest was well into his 60's, and as far as skill level, we had everything from student to surgeon. What was obvious above and beyond these demographic differences, though? *Lifestyle* differences. There were morning people, and then there were *"don't talk to me before I've had a cup of coffee"* people. There were timely people, and then there were *"if you want me to show up on time you'd better tell me we're meeting 15 minutes earlier than we actually are"* people. There were introverted people, and then there were *"Hey, person I barely know! Do you think we're allowed to eat this fruit? Have* **you** *had any diarrhea yet?"* people[1]. Real-life, wholly-different people.

Before we traveled together, our team met on a few occasions to plan and prepare for the journey. These meetings were led by the senior pastor of the church hosting the trip, and one gathering, in particular, pertained mostly to logistics and common courtesies. More so than anything else, the pastor emphasized maintaining a schedule and being where we were expected to be at the time we were expected to be there. He had led dozens of similar trips and said that historically speaking, managing a collective of near strangers on foreign soil was much like—you guessed it—'herding cats'.

I think I actually laughed out loud. I'd never encountered this phrase before, but I could SO picture it. Chaos. Disorder. Squirrelly, little, four-legged critters resisting attempts at being wrangled, and sheer frustration, exhaustion, and exasperation on the part of a wannabe-wrangler.

Because of this warning, I fully expected to witness a bit of cat herding when in Africa. You want to know what actually transpired, though? Order. Much to our leader's admitted surprise and despite our many inherent differences, the team was weirdly well-oiled. We had no problems with tardiness or absenteeism. We did what we came to do, and we did so with almost zero hiccups. Cat herding just wasn't necessary. And the phrase itself? Well, it got stored in the remote corners of my brain where it remained for a few years until something else happened.

Toddlers.

For about three and a half years now, I have lived and breathed cat herding. I have sweat cat herding. I have *cried* cat herding. Flailing of short extremities as they are pulled out from under beds or behind couches when parent and dependent desires don't align, mangy beasts who nearly claw your eyes out at the sight of a bathtub, and sinister stares from glowing eyes as cupfuls of water are ultra-intentionally batted onto the floor. OK…I guess the glowing part is an exaggeration, but only just. You see, guys, toddlers are cats. Unlike their canine counterparts who are easily-trained, loyal, and capable of feeling shame at the sight of their own wrongdoings…felines? Not so much.

Cats have opinions. *Strong* opinions. Cats are emotionally labile and will go from soaking up your snuggles to chewing on your flesh in approximately negative three seconds. On some occasions when the correct form of bribery is dangled in their faces, cats will behave and perform as desired, but on the whole...cats make the rules. Cats do what they want to do on their own terms and in their own good time. They can be oh-so-lazy and oh-so-slow when it's convenient for them, yet can dash from one corner of the house to the other at the blink of an eye to avoid something they perceive as unpleasant.

Why, The World asks, do people still have cats as pets then? Well, they're cute for starters, which is their principal saving grace. Beyond that, though? They're all kinds of hilarious. There are dog people and there are cat people, this we know...but let's be honest. Even the cat haters out there would be liars to deny that they've done some laughing at a viral cat video or two on the internet. You can't not laugh at a cat doing a funny thing.

My home may be cat-free in the literal sense these days, but believe me...I've got cats. Two furballs reside here permanently, and one furball spends 50% of her daytime hours under my care. I am referring to my four-year-old son, Clark, his one-day-older cousin, Madison, and his just-shy-of-three-year-old-sister, Annie. These kiddos are cute and cuddly and super-duper funny, but oh my gravy do they possess all sorts of feline features. They are sassy. They call the shots. They are anything-but-loyal and will turn on you quicker than a cat gets high on catnip. I love this trio fiercely and very willingly set aside my own career and professional ambitions to be a cat herder full-time, but I'd be in straight-up denial to say that doing what I do is fun or rewarding or fulfilling or (yep, I'm going to say it) even *tolerable* all of the time.

Most of the time, being my kids' mom is awesome. *Most* of the time, I find myself wondering what I've done to deserve them and their always-giving, hunky Daddy. *Most* days, I send my husband texts thanking him for working so hard away from home so that I don't have to...and *most* days, I find joy in silly, trivial things like making turkey-shaped muffins or all-green meals. *Some* days, though? Well, some days I send texts to Jonathan reading something more like:

SOS. Send ice cream. Send coffee. Send children who actually listen to their mother occasionally. Send all of the good juju you can muster, and be forewarned that as soon as you get home tonight I'm locking myself in our bedroom. Maybe forever.

What you are about to read is a collection of thoughts, memories, and laughs about the cat-like creatures known as toddlers. It is a tribute to the two I call my own and a way to pay homage to the stage of life that I currently find myself in. The beautiful, crazy, exhausting, amazing, demanding, all-the-things stage. If you've been here before (God bless you!) or are here right now (Godspeed!) or will be here in the future (God save you!)...this is a book for you. If you have no kids or want no kids or are only reading this book to better understand the lives of those around you who do, this is a book for you too. No matter who you are or where you come from, I promise to make you downright chortle a time or two.

But before we get going, a few words: First, let it be known that my loose definition of toddler is a child who is beyond infancy but is not yet in grade school. Basically, I am including children ages one through four in this category. This just so happens to be the ages of the children with whom I reside and over whom I (hardly) rule. Somewhere out there, an individual with degrees and certificates far beyond my own is reading this and would give you a better and more accurate definition. To this, I say: my book, my rules.

Second, just as I spoke in generalizations above about cats, I am going to be making many generalizations about toddlers in the pages to come. I have witnessed with my own eyes the existence of a cat who is always cuddly and would allow himself to be dragged around the house by the tail without a care in the world. Similarly, I have witnessed with my own eyes toddlers who are 99% sweet and amenable. My toddlers are very not this. If yours are, that's totally OK and completely enviable. I hope you'll come along for the ride anyway and laugh at all of the things you don't have to deal with on a daily basis.

Third, I am not a doctor nor a child psychologist nor anything other than a mom who is trying her best and sharing the hilarity of her frequent struggles and occasional successes. Just because something may or may not have worked for me in caring for my own toddlers does not mean that it could or should have the same results for another parent.

Fourth, I 'only' have two children and, therefore, cannot entirely relate to those of you with broods of babes[2]. There may very well be readers with little ones far outnumbering their hands who are tempted to one (or two or three)-up me with their own recollections. Please know that if you are a reader who is almost-literally raising a tribe, I have a deep and sincere and profound respect for you. We are not competitors. We are teammates. We are running the same race with the same goal: to make decent adult human beings out of these tiny people we have to care for.

Fifth, I want to be very clear in reminding both myself and those reading that this work is not meant to be a total bashing of toddlers. More importantly, it is not a blow to the character traits of either of my beautiful, intelligent, strong-willed (we're talking like superhuman strength) children. I am not regretful for one single moment that the task of raising these two lies ahead of me. Instead, I am thankful that I am privileged to have been given it. Having said this, however, those of you who know me or who read my first book know that 'saving face' is not how I roll. While I do promise that I won't use what follows as merely a soapbox for a laundry list of complaints, I will share candidly and honestly and shed light on some memories that others may have opted to simply forget. The truth is that I *want* to remember these moments. I want to remember the good, the bad, the funny, and the challenging. I want to grow and learn as a parent so that my children can learn and grow themselves.

Toddlers require a whole lot of work. Helping to shape and redirect their behaviors is hard. It's like domesticating feral kittens, really. Because they aren't yet old enough to recognize the faults in such thinking, toddlers are essentially self-absorbed, self-protective, tiny-little dictators who truly believe that the world centers around them and their current state of comfort and satisfaction. Honestly, it takes an effort beyond what I have to give as a parent some days. Some days, it feels like whining, crying, questioning, disobeying and flat-out battling trump laughter and joy. On these days, the hard-hard days, the days that don't quite look like storybooks...the bottom line is this: my children are loved, and I love being their mom. They are loved deeply, fully, and without condition...even when their whiskers are showing.

Footnotes

[1] In case you're wondering where I fall...I don't do mornings, I am punctual to a T, and digging a hole and staying inside of it often sounds like a good time to me.

[2] My sisters are of the brood variety, having nine (soon to be 10) kiddos between the two of them. For the record, even they will tell you that I have my hands full.

1 ~~DEMON POSSESSION~~ TANTRUMS

For pretty much my entire life, I've been surrounded by children. My first paid gigs were of the babysitting variety and that stereotypical church volunteer who is always a part of all-things-kid? Well, for years anyway, that was me. Sunday School teacher. Bible School leader. Camp counselor. Nursery volunteer. Yep, yep, yep and yep. I was always humored by tykes, thought I was fairly competent at handling their nonsense, and had enough of a magnetism towards them to result in rock star status when I, Miss Whitney, was spotted at the grocery store.

I came to learn quickly, however, that being around children is not the same as living with a child...especially when that child is as stubborn as all of the mules who have ever walked the Earth combined. While I was in college, my mom and her sister Sharon moved into in-law's quarters attached to the home of my eldest sister and her husband. I semi-lived with Mom and Aunt Sharon—sharing in mealtimes and social aspects of daily life—but their side of the house was without an extra bedroom. Because of this, I had my own room in the main home with Alicia and Joe[1]. Soon after we all moved in and got settled, my sister learned that she was expecting her first child. Tristan Joseph would be welcomed to the world on November 11, 2007. Remember those mules I was talking about? Sit back as I paint a picture for you...

Tristan was an easy-peasy baby who slept through the night at a ridiculously early age. Alicia says it this way:

> **"He was the easiest baby EVER. He slept seven hours straight during the night starting at four weeks. He only ever cried when he needed something, and it was almost always obvious what that something was. He never had 'fussy' times or seemed to get overly stimulated. Getting him on a schedule was a snap…"**

Tristan was cute, he was squishy, and he was intelligent from day one. He was the baby of every parent's dreams. As this little guy grew older, gained independence, and had more to say, however, Alicia and Joe rapidly discovered that the easy-peasy stage was a thing of the past. Days that were once peaceful and predictable and endearing suddenly transitioned to days that were battle-filled and unstable and depleting. So long, sweet baby! Hello, Toddler-Zilla.

Alicia's quote from above? I left it unfinished quite intentionally. Here's how it concludes:

> **"Getting him on a schedule was a snap… Then, he became a toddler and I only felt sane when he was asleep."**

Ha. Ha. Ha. For all that Tristan gifted his parents with in infancy, he mega-made up for during his toddler years. He challenged just about everything that Alicia or Joe asked of him, and I kid you not that for one reason or another— you know, reasons as terrible as being asked to try one small bite of a food he loved—a good 80% of meals concluded with the sound of him screaming. If I'm being honest, a good 80% of *anything*, in fact, ended that way.

Tristan was the master of meltdowns. Like all-out, full-on, Hulk-smash, meltdowns. Kicking walls, beating on closed doors, and yelling that far exceeded the scientific limits of his lung capacity. Don't get me wrong. He had many, many sweet moments, was caught on camera singing the cutest version ever of "Jin-Ga-Boss" (Jingle Bells), and filled his parents' hearts and lives enough that with five children already they are STILL reproducing even today[2]...but Tristan could rage like a champ.

During his toddler years, Tristan even brought challenge to *my* life as his Aunt. He wouldn't be the last child to make me completely lose my crap, but he certainly was the first. And how did this crap-losing event come to be? As I mentioned above, Alicia and Joe continued to procreate despite Tristan's toddler-y ways. They adopted Lilly when Tristan was two and then announced a second pregnancy about 18 months later[3]. To escape the already-existing chaos before adding even more, Alicia and Joe went on a short babymoon, leaving Tristan and Lilly under my care for a portion of the trip. Tristan was newly potty trained at the time, and while some toddlers save their best outbursts for Mom and Dad, oh man did I ever get a potty-related doozy.

Aunt Sharon and I decided to take Tristan on an outing. We ventured to a nearby park and met up with my other sister, Ashley, and her family. Our excursion wasn't spontaneous or haphazard by any means. We were together attending an annual fest, which meant this: people everywhere. The event itself was fun and a good chance for a toddler to breathe in some fresh air. Tristan behaved about as well as could be expected for someone his age, until it was time to go, that is. It was the pack-up, unfortunately, that did us in.

When you've got a potty-training child in tow, pack-up most definitely includes a toilet. Even though he hadn't gone for hours, Tristan wanted precisely zero parts of this idea. I offered use of the private, park-provided bathroom ("*No!*"). I offered use of the toddler toilet I had brought along in the car ("*No!*"), in the bathroom ("*No!*"), or behind a tree ("*No!*"). I even thought I'd be a cool Aunt and offer to let my bud pee *on* a tree ("*Noooooo!*"). I could simultaneously see the temperature of Tristan's blood rising and my patience growing thinner. His screams were getting louder, my face was getting redder, and so many eyes were on us.

Having no idea what more to do, I looked at my Aunt and announced that we were going to put Tristan in a diaper for the ride home. Upon hearing the dreaded D-word, however, Tristan let loose. Everything I had witnessed to that point? That was just the warm-up apparently. He went NUTS. There were occasional slips of sensible phrases including *"I'm not a baby!"*, but mostly what came out of his mouth was just loud-loud, angrier-than-angry nonsense.

Tristan kicked and contorted and made any attempts at diapering him completely impossible. That's when I lost it. In that moment, as I marched a screaming toddler and his clunky potty into the woods for one final attempt at bladder evacuation, I recognized my own loss of control. The truth? The honest, ugly truth? I wanted to hit him.

Feeling what I felt in those chaotic moments scared me and embarrassed me. It was like all of a sudden I could see what was unfolding from outside of my body, remember that I was the adult in the situation, and give credence to the reality that toddlers are just-plain irrational. I won't pretend like I channeled Mister Rogers, talked sense into Tristan, achieved success in toileting, and drove away with a *"Well Done!"* sticker slapped on my chest. Hardly. It was more like I calmed myself down enough not to be arrested and got us all home in one piece. Not exactly a gold medal moment, but success nonetheless.

Toddlers and tantrums are most certainly a package deal, but I don't think any of us quite knew what to do with Tristan's anger. When he would get himself in one of his trademark fits, there just wasn't a thing that could be done to talk him down. We all laugh at it now, Tristan most-especially, but in those days *no one* would have been surprised to see this kiddo land himself in anger management classes as an adult.

Now that I'm a mom with two toddlers of my own, all I can say is this:

Thank. You. Tristan.

Do you recall how I said that being around children wasn't the same as living with children? Well, do you know what's not even close to living with children? *Having* children. As it well should have, becoming a parent changed every aspect of my life. It changed how I looked, how I slept, how I worked, how I felt, how I socialized, how I prioritized, and even how I did marriage. It made me better and far less selfish, but it also made me permanently exhausted.

The newborn days were challenging and required a lot of re-shifting just to navigate the newness of a family of two growing to three and then four. While it's true that those days were made up of never-ending feeding cycles and inevitable infant wails, there were so many moments of stillness and silence in the midst of it all. Very little in life is more precious to me than the memories I have of my newborns lying limp in slumber on my chest. The smells. The warmth. The tiny toes. If I could just bottle that up, oh, how I would.

Toddlerhood is similar to infancy in that while it's magical and completely wonderful from a big-picture perspective, it's challenging and demanding and seemingly endless while you're in it. The difference, though? In my house, anyway, we no longer do 'stillness and silence.' As soon as they could move, my babes were off to the races and never looked back. They didn't want to be held. They didn't want to sit for meals. They didn't want to remain still for stories. They pretty much didn't want to do anything that wasn't their idea or succumb to any polite request the first time (or more like the first *300* times) it was asked. Oh, and tantrums? I think these two were watching Tristan when they were yet eggs in my ovaries.

If it wouldn't have been for living with Tristan and being an eye-witness to his frequent craziness, I think my husband and I may have wondered if an exorcism was in our future. Apparently, Jonathan and I not only breed cats, we breed *rabid* cats. My children are cute and hilarious and sometimes really tender-hearted, but holy cow can they give anyone a run for their money in the tantrum business. My kids can scream with the best of them. My kids can fight with the best of them. In the plainest and best of English, my kids just tantrum real, real good[4].

I remember thinking that having newborns was so hard and for many reasons it really and truly *was* (my first book was entirely about newborn struggles, in fact), but when Clark and Annie shed their infant cocoons and stretched their wings as toddlers? I found myself drinking lots more coffee, sending up lots more Hail Mary's, and honing lots of skills that infancy just never required of me. Skills like bargaining, threatening, yelling, and disciplining. Having toddlers suddenly made having newborns seem easy. It made me miss my unmoving, nonverbal baby blobs. There are lots of things I super-don't miss about having an infant in my home and super-do love about toddlers, but there's something to be said for children who can't yet talk back to you, hit you intentionally, or run away from you when they catch wind of the phrase 'bedtime.'

As compared to the beauty and miracle of infancy as a whole, toddlerhood involves a lot more volatility and tears that go beyond simple needs. Infants cry because they *need* something, usually in the form of food, sleep, comfort, or a new diaper. Toddlers cry because they *feel* something. Toddlers cry because they can.

The way I see it, tantrums are sort of the physical culmination of the cat-like tendencies toddlers possess. Toddlers like to have things their way, do things in their own time, and remain 103 percent comfortable always. When any of those things don't happen, toddlers lack the restraint and the logic to respond rationally. Hence, they respond in an opposite fashion. They respond erratically, emotionally, physically or whatever-else-ally serves as a release in that moment.

So, when you're sitting outside on a warm day enjoying the sounds of a nearby woodpecker who suddenly stops tapping…an adult wouldn't throw herself down on the driveway and refuse to go indoors until said woodpecker could be heard again. A toddler named Annie, though? Yep, she would. Or when you've just had a splinter removed from your palm…an adult wouldn't burst into tears unless, perhaps, the process caused a whole lot of discomfort. But a toddler? Well, a toddler named Clark once cried after such a removal not because he was in any sort of pain but because he wanted his splinter *back*. These responses are not rational, because toddlers are not rational beings. As adults, we know the difference between how we *should* react and how we *want* to react to situations that suck[5]. Toddlers don't.

For fun, I polled my own friends and family and asked them to share with me their funniest experiences with tantrums. I took those responses and have compiled for you a list of real-life reasons for some of (predominantly) Pennsylvania's finest fits:

-Socks that felt like knives (Angie)

-Spoons that were the wrong color (Erin)

-Being deprived of one's right to play in a full-of-trash
    trashcan (Laura)

-The realization that the crackers being hand-fed to
    the dog were not coming back (Natasha)

-M&M's gone too soon (Amy)

-Pacifiers out of reach because they were thrown by
    the same someone demanding reunification (Kait)

-New pajamas that missed the mark on acceptable use
    of patterns (Josh)

-Public restrooms without "appetizers" [hand
    sanitizer] (Bethany)

-A worldwide shortage of warm popsicles (Matt)

-Being left bereft and alone in the world when one's
    moldy "pet" avocado was thrown away (Emily)

-The tortured spot between losing a sock, wanting it
back on, and prohibiting this from happening
(April)

-Cruel parents that wouldn't allow their child to eat
the remnants of a popped balloon (Kirsten)

-Body proportions that prohibited fitting inside of toy
castles and toy cars (Rebecca)

-The revelation that a toy T-Rex was not, indeed, a
"real" pet (Colley)

-The assumption that all human beings want to eat
bananas without peels (Jamy)

-Ears that declined kisses (Stacey)

-Being freed from the time-out corner [yep, FREED]
(Robin)

-Evil sock seams (Suzi)[6]

And the clincher:

-Being denied the right to visualize an empty cheese
wrapper before it was tossed in the garbage (Sharon)

Oh, the humanity.

Meltdowns of the toddler sort can be all over the map.
Occasionally, they can even be tender and happen for sweet or heart-wrenching reasons like receiving hard-to-swallow news. To illustrate, consider the following example shared with me by a friend. When her daughter Taylor was at an age and maturity level enough to understand the truth, Andrea was asked whether or not Santa was real. Andrea delicately explained that, no, he was not a real person

and although the disclosure seemed a bit saddening to Taylor, it was taken in stride. When she thought a moment further, however, and asked if that meant that a certain bunny and fairy were also fictitious—well—it was just too much. Tender tantrum.

Tantrums can also be instigated. If you've never before watched Jimmy Kimmel's late-night show, a really, really good day to give it a gander is the day after Halloween. On an annual basis, Jimmy asks parent viewers to video tape themselves professing untruthfully to their young children that they've eaten every last piece of trick-or-treat treasure. It's completely awful, but it's SO funny. From my own personal circle, a long-time friend, LeeAnn, shared with me a similar experience. Upon making a pitstop for drinks at a gas station, LeeAnn's then three-year-old son, Eli, requested chocolate milk. This request was seemingly simple until the friend of a much-older sibling informed Eli that there was no more chocolate milk in the whole world. Being the awesome parent that she is, LeeAnn played along (ha!), and informs me that Eli's reaction was in the 'the world is ending' category and that this was *"the saddest cry I think he has ever had."* In Eli's defense, good chocolate milk really is something special[7]. Instigated tantrum.

In whatever form or fashion they take, tantrums are basically just nonsensical reactions to the happenings of the world. I had a lot of folks chime in on this topic and received many responses that made me giggle or nod my head like *"yep!"*, but my favorite meltdown-inducing reason of them all was this:

"He wanted ice water. So I gave him ice water."
(Courtney)

So, completely signature in the land of toddlers. You hear their demands, you meet their demands, and you receive compensation in the form of emotional or physical abuse. You've just gotta love these silly, ridiculous, critters.

When you're parenting a toddler and are knee-deep in the muck of tantrums, the fitful moments can feel unending. They can become so much a part of what you do on a daily basis that your husband can return home from work, ask you how your day was, and leave you saying *"Great!"*... because in all honesty you totally forgot that your daughter had screamed something fierce for a solid 20 minutes before nap for next to no reason at all (which maybe just happened today...). The fitful moments can feel embarrassing. They can feel draining. They can make all of the tiny steps forward in demonstrating kindness or self-control or consideration get lost and forgotten and overlooked. I'll be the first one to admit that sometimes I get so caught up in the things I wish my kids would do better that I miss their growth. I miss the awesome things they *do* do.

Tantrums at home after a long day of battles, *"no's"*, and one too many displays of deliberate defiance suck. Tantrums in the middle of the grocery store with 100 sets of strangers' eyes watching and a cartful of yet-to-be-paid-for items suck. Tantrums at a summer cookout surrounded by dozens of well-meaning family members with offers of *"Oh, honey you've just got to..."* suck. Tantrums aren't fun, and they aren't glamorous, and they aren't as often the tender or hilarious sort as much as they are the *I. Can't. Even.* sort. But you know what? They're purposeful.

Purposeful? Really? Toddler meltdowns may feel like the furthest thing from purposeful when you're mustering all of your strength just to abate and survive one without a prison sentence to face. Even with older toddlers under our roof, I promise that we do lots of surviving over here some days. Thankfully, however, I am still able to see the bigger workings at play. The violent tantrums, the loud tantrums, the tender tantrums, and the downright silly tantrums? They're just an often-exhausting part of learning. Tantrums happen because toddlers are processing the world around them, the feelings they are just beginning to recognize, and the newly discovered skills that will ultimately benefit them. It'd be way-cool if such learning was a once and done thing, and maybe for some toddlers it is, but in my home anyway, appropriate demonstrations of independence, autonomy, and decision making simply take time. Over and over and over and over and over and over and over again time.

The beauty of it all is that even the stubbornest of toddlers can turn into the coolest of cats as older children, teenagers, and adults...and thank the Good Lord for that. Remember Tristan, that mule in toddler form? He's always been great and worth every bit of effort, but now he's these things in non-screaming form. Tristan is a calm, thoughtful, smart-smart young man who believes in transparency and bettering himself even when it's hard. He's still stubborn like his mom because it's core to his nature, but OH, how far he has come from those toddler days.

Thanks to Tristan and the countless other adults who were once jerky, challenging, hostile little youngsters, I'm confident that my children are going to be influencers in society someday. I'm confident that all of this honing of less-than-desirable behavior will ultimately result in great stuff. Ask anyone. My kids are deeply funny and incredibly perceptive. They're already awesome, and when the day comes that we make it an entire 24 hours (right now I'd take *one*...) without a parent-targeted mutiny? Clark and Annie will be even awesome-er.

And until that day? Well, until that day we'll continue to have two-year-olds who remove their socks and shoes in the car on a frigid winter day despite repeated requests not to do so, stand barefooted in the garage screaming because their feet are cold, and refuse to take the three steps required to enter the warm house. Oh, toddlers.

Footnotes

[1] Actually, I had two rooms. One for sleeping and one for lounging in front of the TV. Then, along came a baby, and suddenly my TV room was lost forever. It appears that children were ruining my life even before I had my own. Kidding, kidding!!

[2] At present, Alicia and Joe have five children and are expecting their sixth. Tristan is 11, Lillian is 10, Sydney is 7, their twins, Julia and Zander, are 3, and baby Zoey is scheduled to arrive in just a little over two months. Lilly was welcomed into our family via international adoption from China, and Julia, Zander, and Zoey are embryo adoptions. Look it up! It's

something that so many folks are unaware of, and I applaud Alicia and Joe for their hearts for these babies who otherwise wouldn't have had a chance at life. My sister is truly a hero of mine, and both a nutter and a saint wrapped into one, hot package. In case you were wondering, she's totally rocking pregnancy at the age of 40. She'd tell you otherwise, but she'd be wrong...

[3] Fun fact #1: Alicia and Joe's second daughter, Sydney, arrived exactly on Tristan's fourth birthday. Fun fact #2: Alicia is Type A to the max and believes in controlling every situation. She felt strongly that her children should each have their own birthday. Because of this, when Alicia went into labor with Sydney she pretended she didn't...for hours. We were all not-so-gently telling her that willpower alone is not enough to keep a child from being born on the living room floor. Eventually, she relented and arrived at the hospital very much in labor. Sydney was born at 10:27 PM. Sorry, Alicia. As the saying goes...close only counts in horseshoes and hand grenades!

[4] At this point, I must speak to those of you who know my children and have only seen them in their best, cherubic, hysterical-in-a-good-way form. I fully acknowledge that I have been blessed with super-funny kids who have a habit of making everyone they meet fond of them. I also acknowledge that (Hallelujah and Amen!) Clark and Annie reserve about 90% of their misbehavior for those times they are at home and with Jonathan and/or me. Please know, however, that this is a ruse. The immediate neighbors can attest that some days, more screaming than laughter emanates from our home. Trust me.

[5] Even as adults, it's sometimes difficult not to give in to how we want to react. My best illustration of this is road rage. You know those times when another driver does something incredibly stupid and renders you uncharacteristically angry, hostile, and violent? For some reason, I think vehicles bring out the toddler in everyone. Even those adults who always respond as they should in face to face exchanges will occasionally slip and respond as they want to behind the wheel. A primo example of this is my own husband. Jonathan is about the single nicest and calmest person on planet Earth. In a car though...not even close.

[6] Is anyone else taking note of the sock trend? Toddlers and socks, apparently, are nature's enemies.

[7] If and when your travels bring you to York, Pennsylvania, do yourself a favor and grab some chocolate milk from Perrydell Farm. Best everrrrrr.

2 "NO!" AND OTHER SUPER-FUN THINGS THAT TODDLERS SAY

A few nights ago, I was sitting on the couch snuggled up with my favorite three people in the world watching Disney's *Mulan*. It was a typical-yet-perfect family movie night done in Bausman style. Sleeping bags on the couch. Popcorn with M&M's in bowls. Good, good stuff. We had almost reached the end of the movie and (spoiler alert) made it to the pivotal point in which Mulan shifts from a young lady overstepping her place in society to a heroine who has saved her entire nation. If you've never seen it, the scene is quintessential Disney. It's reflective, it's inspirational, and it makes you get all sappy inside and goosebumpy outside. Clark and Annie had never before seen *Mulan*, and for two toddlers who haven't quite yet learned the art of sitting still for anything—movies included—they were pretty well taken in and uncharacteristically quiet. Until the following line was spoken, that is:

> **Take this so your family will know what you have done for me...and this, so the world will know what you have done for China[1].**

Upon hearing the Emperor make this statement, our littlest pip-squeak's mouth curled up in the most devilish of grins. Being her parents and knowing full-well how Annie's brain works, Jonathan and I locked eyes, raised eyebrows, and did that telepathic spouse thing that we do. We didn't say a word, yet we both knew and acknowledged that we knew what was coming next.

"Daddy, he said buh-jigh-nuh!"

If you and I aren't on the same page, I'll give you just a moment to read the quote above out loud. Sound it out. There you go! Now I think you've got it. Oh, Annie. That would *not* be what the Emperor said. He said *Chi*na.

Fortunately for me, my kids are downright hilarious and say things much like this often enough to keep me sane and laughing in between their meltdowns. Not all of the things they say, however, are so well received. Like all toddlers, my kids have go-to phrases which are shouted or declared a good 600 times a day. These phrases don't make me laugh. They make my eyes twitch and my blood pressure rise. Here is a short-list version of some of the things my children say that get (way, way) under my skin along with 'fun' examples of their usage.

<u>No!</u>

'No' has got to be the single word my children use most. Sometimes, in fact, they unleash it even before their ears have registered what is being said to them. My kids just like to go against the grain...no matter what the grain may be. Because of this, 'no' is more like a reflex than an actual conscious choice of word use. They're so used to saying (or screaming) 'no' at Jonathan and me, that we have to laugh when they occasionally do it out of habit and then catch themselves, like this:

JONATHAN: Would you guys want to stop for ice cream on the way home?

CLARK: No! Wait—yes! Yes, Daddy, yes!!

In their defense, I think 'no' is one of the words *I* use most too…

Give me/get me…!

In the next chapter, we'll talk at length about how being the caretaker of a toddler closely mirrors being the servant of a demanding egomaniac. For now, however, I'll say this: I really and truly don't mind helping my kids and serving my kids because I realize that at two and four years old, there are things that they simply cannot do on their own. For reasons of safety or coordination or whatever else, lots of things just aren't doable for Clark and Annie. What I *do* mind, however, is being tyrannized. If I am asked nicely, there is very little that I wouldn't do for my children…even when it inconveniences me. If I am brashly commanded to do something, though? Well, my natural response to *that* is not usually a "*Sure thing, sweetie!*" It's more like an "*Excuse me? How about we try that again.*" My kids do a whole heck of a lot of trying again these days. 'Give me' and 'get me' just don't sit well with Mommy or Daddy around here.

I can do it myself!

Part of the beauty of toddlerhood is the development of independence, but it's also part of the struggle. A big, ugly part. Having "*I can do it myself!*" toddlers like I do often means taking double the time to brush teeth, double the time to get in and out of the car, and double the time to get dressed. It means having double the stains and double the injuries. For me as a mom, it means finding the balance between asserting myself as an authority when it is necessary and relenting control so that my little ones can learn and grow. It is succumbing to mismatched outfits and shirts worn backwards even in public. It is watching Annie spin around and around and around in a circle, much like a cat chasing its tail, to get her second arm in the coat. It is also why a certain little boy comes home from the Crayola Experience with a crayon named 'xbdddjhhhhh'.

I don't want to!

Lots of times throughout the day, I intentionally give my children choices. It may be what shirt they'd like to wear, what color plate they'd like to use, or what type of fruit they'd like to have with their breakfast. Ultimately, providing choices is a good thing and helps to foster decision making skills and gives my rascals a sense of involvement in the happenings of their world. Lots and lots of times throughout the day, however, I super-intentionally *don't* give my children choices. Number one, *I'm* the boss (don't I wish). Number two, choices take time. Number three, *I'm* the boss. Yep, I know I already said that. It's just very, very not true a lot of the time and I thought that maybe if I put it out there again I would believe it. One can dream…Anyway, let's just say that Jonathan and I hear the phrase *"I don't want to!"* often. Whether it's after being told that bath time awaits, that it's time for bed, or heck, even that it's time to eat a desserts-only dinner, my kids are just good at not wanting involvement in any idea that isn't their own. Because of this, one could create a drinking game out of how many times I say *"I'm not asking. I'm telling."* on a daily basis.

Pleeeeeeeeeeease!

Please is a confusing word. Usually, it's something you want your kids to say. It's one of the first basic uses of manners that is instilled in the brains of little ones. We even taught our two the sign for 'please' before their vocal cords made sounds more coordinated than babbles, squeals, and coos. Like many children, however, Clark and Annie have mastered the art of begging. Because of this, the word please is more frequently used as a bargaining device than as a display of politeness in our home. More often than it makes me proud or agreeable to a request, 'please' makes me cringe. With Clark especially, it's like a crescendo. He is inhumanely denied something he *needs*—like Skittles for breakfast—and the ascent begins.

> **"But Mommy, please!" [A little louder] "Please Mommy! [Louder still] "Please, please, please?" [And...we're there] "PLEEEEEEEEEEEASE!"**

'Please' and I go from BFF's to mortal enemies pretty often. Sometimes, I long for it and say things like "*...and what word is missing?*" when I am handed yet another please-less demand. Other times, though, I loathe it and say things like "*No means no. No doesn't mean we say please one hundred times. If I hear it again, I will box you up and ship you to Texas.*" Calm down, I would never ship my children to Texas. Maryland, maybe, but...KIDDING.

All of these short, little phrases eat away at my patience nibble by nibble on a daily basis. Very intentionally, I start the majority of my days about an hour before my kids' feet hit the ground. I love sleep more than I can express to you, and if there were no other variables to consider, I would always choose the warmth of my bed and an indefinite death to all alarm clocks over contributing to society. Since there *are* other variables, however—predominantly two living, breathing, terrorizing-their-adult-housemates variables—I rise early. I do this because when those cute little paws touch down, they hit the ground running.

If you've ever met my children, you'll agree that they have a lot to say. Annie almost always, and Clark as soon as he feels comfortable in his surroundings. Annie is an 'I'll say whatever thought crosses my mind' kind of girl[2], and Clark is an 'I'll ask 14 questions a second to figure out how all things have ever worked' kind of guy. While these qualities are central to who my kids are and qualities that endlessly entertain Jonathan and me, they are also qualities that are a tad (ha) abrasive first thing in the morning. On the days I *don't* get out of bed and pull myself together before my children make an appearance, things look and sound a little bit like this:

<<My eyes jolt open as the bedroom door is flung wide>>

CLARK: Hi Mommy! It's time to get up. My clock says 'seven zero zero'. I woke up when it said 'six zero five' but I stayed in my room until the light came on. What are we having for breakfast, Mommy? Does Madison come today, Mommy? Can I stay in my pajamas today? Can I wear these pajamas again tonight? Is today a preschool day, Mommy? Can I open the container of vitamins today?

<<I groan and stretch>>

ME: Hi bud. How about...

CLARK: Are you ready to go downstairs, Mommy?

ME: Let me...

CLARK: Ooo, can we have waffles today Mommy? And I can put peanut butter on top and whatever kind of sprinkles I want? I want the cube ones. But I'll put them on myself. Does that sound good, Mommy? I don't think Annie will want the cube ones. Maybe she can choose the heart ones. Mommy, can Annie choose the heart ones?

ME: Sounds good, bud. But let's…

CLARK: Mommy, I think I hear Annie. We should open her door and see if she's awake. Can I get her Mommy? Well, she can come out when she's ready. Come on, Mommy! Let's go downstairs. Mommy, come on!

<<I am taken by the arm, indelicately assisted out of bed, and now trudge stiffly down the stairs. Using the bathroom or brushing my teeth will have to wait…>>

Maybe it's just because they're children and have energy enough to power a large city, but from the first second my kids' eyes open in the morning, they are ready to go, go, go[3]. Mommy, however, isn't. Mommy needs time to accept that sleeping forever is, sadly, not an option. Mommy needs time to process things more complicated than pushing the start button on the coffee maker. When Mommy gets up before the kids do, this happens much more smoothly and with much less crankiness. When Mommy gets up before the kids do, she's armed with two essential weapons before she lays eyes on their angelic faces and is bombarded with their immediate questions. First, a bloodstream that contains caffeine[4]. Second, a stomach that contains food.

Hungry and/or groggy Whitney are the least friendly versions of me. Just ask my husband. Yesterday, actually, I compared myself to a delicate flower, and Jonathan's response? *"More like a cactus."* Thanks, love. I'm going to pretend he was referring to the fact that I have very poor self-care practices and haven't shaved my legs for three weeks. His comment, however, had nothing to do with shaving or a lack thereof. If you've had the unfortunate experience of meeting me for the first time when I was in either my hungry or my sleepy state, I do apologize. I can't be held accountable for the things I say when my blood sugar is unstable or my level of alertness is not at its peak. I've gone in spurts of returning to my love of sleep and letting the kids wake me every morning, but I simply need that bit of 'me time' before the demands, and the questions, and the rebuttals, and just alllll the words—even the four-letter variety—start coming my way.

Under my roof, I swear that some days a solid 90% of the sentences spoken by my toddlers contain choice 'four-letter words.' Since Jonathan and I aren't swearers—except for an occasional use for comedic purposes, anyway—we're talking *these* bad boys: 'poop,' 'butt,' and 'toot.' Like many kids their age, Clark, Annie, and Madison find pure joy in all things rear-related. No lie, they could talk for hours about this stuff. They ask questions about poop. They tell stories about poop. They play games that involve poop. I kid you not that if Annie finds herself at an atypical loss for words, she very literally smiles and just says *"poopy diaper."* It's almost like her Tourette tic, and it's one part frustrating, one part embarrassing, and one part hysterical.

To demonstrate fully just how core 'potty words' are to Annie's existence, I purchased a cheap tally ticker online and made an experiment out of my youngest child's vocabulary. From the time she woke in the morning until she was laid down for bed that night, I made an intentional point of counting just how often the words 'butt,' 'poop,' or 'toot' escaped her lips. The grand total? 71 times. Let's say it again. Seventy. One. Keep in mind that this is only a count of the times I actually heard her say these words. Annie talked to herself in her room for 30 plus minutes before nap time and bedtime and was out of earshot and off playing with her brother and cousin for one or two good hours. I can only imagine the heights of the real count. Perhaps next time I'll try renting one of those police force body cams for her to wear. Bodily functions and body parts just seem to be ringers when it comes to the things that make my toddlers' wheels turn.

Toddlers say all sorts of things. They say funny things. They say awkward things. They say frustrating things. And…they say *honest* things. Like, honest-honest. If they think it, they say it because much like inebriated adults, toddlers lack a filter. Getting a compliment from a toddler in any fashion is a big deal simply because they aren't capable of flattery for the sake of sparing one's feelings. If they tell you that they like the lunch you prepared for them, it's because they really do. If they tell you that you look beautiful, it's because they really believe it. Compliments from toddlers, however, are much fewer and further between than comments that are quite the opposite in nature. Critical, pointed, offensive, inconsiderate and sometimes downright embarrassing comments just come naturally from tots. Comments like *"Daddy has a biiiiig belly!"* (not true) or *"Mommy, this dinner is disgusting"* (sometimes true). We hear lots of those unfortunately.

The Queen of funny-slash-inappropriate comments in public is my niece, Madison. Her parents would be the first to tell you this and have been gracious enough to give me the go ahead to share it with you. In terms of toddlers, Madison is a gem. She is eager to please, a superb helper, and has the biggest heart. She wears it on her sleeve so much, in fact, that Annie or Clark crying for any reason brings her to tears…even if she is completely uninvolved. While she has her moments like any child and has learned a thing or two about raging meltdowns from my own fluff balls, we used to call her the dream toddler because of the way she handled tantrums. Madison would just 'plank'[5]. Quite contrary to the stereotypical images of toddler tantrums with screaming and flailing about, Madison would get upset, drop to the ground in silent tears, suck her thumb, and lay as stiff as a board for minutes. It was so funny.

From the time they were babies, Madison was always 'easier' than Clark. She stayed put where you sat her while Clark climbed bookshelves. While Madison flirted with strangers and loved family gatherings, Clark cried if and when someone even looked at him the wrong way, and got overwhelmed and overstimulated at get-togethers. Madison's social butterfly tendencies, however, are what lead this little lass to have loose lips. Madison thrives in social settings and is comfortable enough to say whatever crosses her mind no matter who is around. Unlike Clark who probably has many uncouth thoughts in public yet never speaks them because he is introverted and more of a thinker, Madison's thoughts are spoken regardless of her surroundings. So when she's at the store with Savanna and Justin and spots someone with bright pink hair walking by, Madison doesn't just think *"Ewwww! I don't like her hair!"* Nope, she says it. Loudly. Oh, toddlers[6].

Dealing appropriately with all of the things that toddlers say on a daily basis can be exhausting. Some days, that exhaustion may come from the outright fits of laughter that toddler talk initiates, but some days it comes from fighting constant battles. It takes a lot of energy to acknowledge and redirect the inappropriate, demanding, or unkind things that so often escape their mouths. It also takes a lot of energy to mindfully choose what comes out of our own as parents and role models. Chances are if I say it, so will my kids. Occasionally, this results in my little ones saying things far beyond their age and maturity level like *"Clarky, that's not a-pwo-pree-wit* (appropriate)", or cute things like *"Good job, Mommy! That's my girl. I'm so proud of you!"*…but often it results in them saying things like *"I **hate** when…"* or *"What the…?"*[7]. Oops. Could be a whole lot worse, I know, but my toddlers make lots of these little slips on a daily basis that necessitate a reexamination of my own verbiage.

A rapidly expanding vocabulary is one of the hallmark pieces of toddlerhood. Under typical conditions, toddlers enter this developmental stage with only a handful of basic words in their tool belt. When they exit it, though? They have heaps of words to call upon. While it's true that these 'cats' use some (OK...a lot) of their words to hiss and spit, it's the *other* words—the words that are used for saying incredibly cool and loving things, the words that make your heart explode as a parent—that make it all worthwhile. Like the first time that pint-sized terror looks you in the eye and says *"I love you"* not because he can but because he understands its meaning and really feels it? That's the stuff right there, guys.

For all of the less-than-desirable and hard-to-hear-100-times-a-day statements that my children make, they really and truly do say some awesome stuff too. Sometimes it's just super funny stuff, like the invention of new words or random nonsense that even the most mature of parents couldn't not laugh at. Examples? Two of Annie's go-to, self-established words are to'morning (tomorrow morning) and yesternight (yesterday night). In case you're lacking clarity on these, I'll use them in sentence form just as Annie did recently.

> **"Momma, do you remember where we went yesternight? The birthday party!"** [I did remember]

AND

> **"Momma, can I have Chips Ahoy for breakfast to'morning?"** [The answer, just in case you're wondering, was yes. Yes, indeed, Annie had Chips Ahoy for breakfast the following morning.]

These are good, I'll give it to her—so good, in fact, that I just discovered yesternight is a legitimate word—but I'll let you in on one that is even better. On more than one occasion, Annie has referred to an eyebrow as an eye-stache. I dare you to see an eyebrow as just an eyebrow ever, ever again. Words like these give me the giggles every time, and let's be honest...they make all of the sense in the world.

Sometimes, the things my kids say aren't exactly funny, but they just make me stand back and beam with pride. Like '*how did I create such a cool human being?*-level pride. The day that Clark requested a cup of coffee (decaf, of course) on his own for the first time and stopped me from putting chocolate milk in it by saying, *"Nah, just plain!"* Well you can imagine that I had tears in my eyes that day. That's *my* son! Ha.

All joking aside, my toddlers say some pretty profound things too. They think and they feel and they process the happenings of the world, and sometimes this culminates in ultra-tender conversations. One night during our bedtime routine, I prayed aloud for a friend who had lost a baby girl, a friend for whom my heart was heavy. This is how Clark took in and responded to that prayer:

CLARK: Mommy, why did her baby get lost?

ME: Well, honey, she didn't 'get' lost. She died. Sometimes when a person says they 'lost' someone, it means that that person died and isn't with them anymore. It makes people very sad when someone dies.

CLARK: But, Mommy, she doesn't have to be sad!

ME: Why is that, bud?

CLARK: Well, if her baby died, she just has to get it a new battery. That would make her happy again!

Oh, my sweet and perceptive boy. In Clark's world, a world in which toys die and are brought back to life with the replacement of worn-out batteries, he offered his sensible solution. How simple and precious it was, and how it choked me up. Conversations like these aren't easy by any means and I'm sure that how I respond in those moments is usually not textbook or 'right' or even what is most helpful to my children in the moment, but I love even having the chance to get it wrong. I love that Clark and Annie are at an age now where they can say these things and hear what Jonathan and I have to say in response. I love that we can help shape how they see the world and how they relate to those around them. Big stuff. Important stuff. Cool stuff.

My toddlers have a lot to say. A lot and a lot and a lot, lot, lot of words to say. I'll take all of the demanding and selfish words, I'll take all of the inappropriate words, I'll take all of those little phrases that often brings me to my wits' end, and I'll mold them for good. I'll continue to put in the effort, I'll continue to navigate my way through the commands, and—honestly—I'll still stuff my face in a pillow from time to time and have a good scream…but I'll do it because the growth of my children is worth it to me and to the world.

Footnotes

[1] *Mulan*. Directed by Tony Bancroft and Barry Cook, Walt Disney Pictures, 1998.

[2] We joke that Annie's picture should be featured next to the definition of 'flight of ideas' in mental health textbooks.

[3] One qualification is necessary here, however. When my children wake on their own, they are ready to go, go, go. Clark, however, possesses my disdain for being awakened. While Annie is typically fairly even-keeled regardless of how or when she wakes, Clark is not usually a happy nor even a tolerable camper when the tables turn and we have to wake him for one reason or another. To this, I say "Karma, my dear son".

[4] I would argue, however, that the caffeine itself isn't what fuels me. Don't get me wrong, I'm totally addicted to it and get one of those naggy-annoying headaches if I don't drink it every morning, but unless I'm drinking a venti dark roast with an added shot or two of espresso, I don't get a jolt of energy from caffeine or even a boost most days. For me, it's just the coffee. I love, love coffee. The darker and blacker and Starbucks-ier the better. The first sip of my morning coffee is one of those things that literally gives me pause and makes me say "mmmmmmm". I love the routine of waking up to something I enjoy so deeply each and every day. (And if a Starbucks employee is reading this and wants to make me a paid spokesperson or send free samples my way, I am very OK with this…Just sayin'.)

[5] …And all of The Office superfans out there will now go back and watch the season eight premier yet again. You're welcome.

[6] If you're thinking that this is one area in which, perhaps, my toddlers have spared me…think again. Annie is going to follow very closely in her big cousin's shoes. How she hasn't totally embarrassed Jonathan and me yet outside of our home is beyond me.

[7] They don't know what comes next…promise.

3 BECOMING CINDERELLA

My mother-in-law is currently in the process of moving. As she makes her way through items that have been stashed away for quite some time, she decides what she does and doesn't want to hold onto and then passes anything relating to Jonathan our way so that we can make the final determination as to its destiny. If you know me—as she well does—most of these things eventually find themselves at home in the trash can. Before this, however, they provide for entertainment, reminiscence, and laughs. A few weeks back, Annie and I were looking through some old books that Mom had found packed up in her basement. They were books from Jonathan's childhood, and many were the typical picture book style that toddlers love best.

Annie was flipping through the pages of a depiction of *Cinderella*, and while she knows this character in her fanciest, most put-together, trademark-gown-donning form, it was an illustration of her in her raggedy, tattered maid's attire that puzzled my daughter. When Annie pointed to the picture and asked, *"Who's that, momma?"*, I took a break from the book in my own hands and looked where her little finger had landed. What I saw was an image of a weary-looking young woman on her hands and knees scrubbing a dirty floor. In the background, her step-sisters stood idly and schemed how best to make their next mess. Without hesitation, I chuckled and responded

"*Well… that's me!*" I may not have evil stepsisters, but I do indeed have ~~evil~~ scheming toddlers.

There is no doubt that having a child and embarking on the journey of parenthood is an exhilarating experience. On one side of the coin, being given a human life to foster and protect and enrich is invigorating and actually breathes wind into the sails of a mom or a dad. Before I became a parent, I was certainly alive, but in many ways I feel like my life really began the day I gave birth to Clark. I never knew what it was like to love something so deeply, to have such a clear purpose beyond myself, and to feel like I could live on long after my finite body fails in doing right by this little person.

On the opposite side of the very same coin, however, being responsible for all of these things—hugely important things like nourishment, well-being, growth, and development—is draining. Putting someone else's needs above your own every minute of every day is exhausting. It requires double the effort, double the time, and double the sweat…and that's only factoring in the addition of *one* other person to care for. A lot of the time for me, those efforts are quadrupled because I have four people to keep alive: Annie, Clark, Madison, and myself. Those of you brooders out there? Your efforts are likely sky-high. For as harsh as it sounds, having a child draws parallels to servanthood in many regards. I may have a flair for dramatic prose and exaggeration, but it's the honest to goodness truth.

Think about it. A woman's body is at the beck and call of her developing babe when she's pregnant. What she eats, what she drinks, and what activities she participates in all revolve around that bulging bump. A momma-to-be doesn't get to choose what nutrients she does or doesn't share with the tiny roommate her body is subletting to. Not at all. Growing fetuses simply take what they need. And then, when those seven pounds of squish are born into the world (another process over which a woman has very little say), she remains captive to hormones and lactation and a hungry belly for months on end.

When a woman's body is no longer serving as an incubator or a milk factory, I'll give it to you that this is, perhaps, a shifting point in servanthood…but it is certainly not the end of it. Being the parent of a toddler is very much an extension of this service. Day after day after day. Between meal preparation, cleaning up incessant messes, trying to maintain some semblance of a household, providing constant entertainment, and attending to matters of hygiene, it's a servant's kind of life for sure. It's an others-first, *"I'll eat if there's time or anything left"*, 'clean' no longer lasts more than five minutes, kind of life. Together, let's unwrap the servant-like components of caring for toddlers. In doing so, I'll be able to give you a tour of my home and a look into my cat-herding life. To begin, let's start with the inevitable when it comes to toddlers: messes.

Do you recall that I mentioned having *"I can do it myself!"* toddlers? Well, allow me to clarify and note that this is always the case when *"I can do it myself!"* stalls bedtime, bath time, or being stuck in the car. I do not, however, have *"I can do it myself!"* toddlers when 'doing it thyself' involves cleaning up messes. Clark is the King of creating messes that he wants nothing to do with when playtime is over. Messes are very much a part of our everyday—more like every minute—life. Legos here, there and everywhere…like, in my bed everywhere. Water covering every sink top and bathroom floor. Closets and drawers emptied of their clothing contents. *Every* puzzle piece in the entire house thrown into one large and daunting heap. Finger-paint on walls and faucets and faces instead of on paper. Grapes plucked one by one from the stems and tossed lovingly onto the kitchen floor only to be not-so-lovingly squashed. Yep, we do messes.

For a lot of bad reasons, today is a good day to write about cleaning up after my children. Before I reveal to you those 'bad reasons', however, you'll need just a little bit of background information. I am a neat freak and find that tidying both soothes my soul and appeases my OCD tendencies. If my house doesn't appear orderly, I can very much guarantee you that I am not relaxed. My sisters and husband make fun of me for this regularly and assure me that I invest far too much brain power in caring about such things, but I am who I am. This being said, however, please know that I am not a *clean* freak. There's a distinct difference. I straighten constantly and pick up toys constantly and do a lot of surface level cleaning. Real cleaning, though—like actual mopping and vacuuming that involves moving things instead of just working around them—does not take place as often. Wear white socks around my home for a few minutes or take a peek under my couch, and you'll see what I mean.

Even mere surface level cleaning is a time-consuming process involving creativity when it's done in the presence of toddlers. Typically, I sequester mine in a still-messy room until the one I'm working on looks decent, move on to the next location, and look back five seconds later to discover that the natives grew restless in their assigned spot and have already trashed the one that had been 'clean'. Today, however, was a deep clean day. Deep clean days are like surface level cleaning on crack. We're talking moving around furniture and dusting off ceiling fans that have collected about an inch of dust. Deep clean days only happen a few days a year…like the day after your four-year-old discovers pieces of cereal on the floor and says to you "*Woah! We haven't even had this cereal in ages.*" Can it, Clark.

I started deep clean day upstairs while Clark and Annie finished their breakfast in front of the television (feel free to judge). For the few moments they were still, there was peace. It would have been oh-so-easy to keep that TV on and allow the brains of my little ones to be held captive, but instead I powered off the tube, set the captives free, and told them that if they wanted any screen time before nap they'd have to earn it by playing nicely while I cleaned. I'm not entirely sure how my children interpreted 'nicely' at two and four years old, but I didn't quite receive their efforts in a sugar and spice kind of way.

The first hiccup: tissues. For as necessary of a staple as tissues are, tissues drive me crazy. Annie is drawn to tissues like a moth to a flame and it absolutely makes me nuts. In Annie's world, tissues aren't for blowing noses. Oh, no. Tissues are for making snowballs. Tissues are for choreographing ribbon dances. Tissues are for decorating! Because of this, tissue boxes in our home have to be cleverly placed in spots that are out of a certain little girl's reach. A few places you can currently locate tissues? Hiding in closets, perched atop medicine cabinets, and serving as makeshift art forms on the walls. If we don't get creative, tissues end up everywhere. Today, the Tissue Tosser struck again. Thinking that our littlest one might have reached an age or have been sternly spoken to about tissue waste enough times for things to sink in, Jonathan and I tried again to keep them in plain sight. In our master bedroom, we had one box of tissues on Jonathan's nightstand and one on mine. Well, guess what I got to halt my cleaning efforts for first? Yep. Picking up two entire boxes' worth of tissues from behind my very-heavy bed.

The second hiccup: sprinkles. Yes, sprinkles. My children are obsessed, probably to an unhealthy level, with sprinkles. In fact, they bedazzle their waffles to a height that would blind a unicorn. I know, I know—sugar, food dye, blah, blah, blah—and I'm sorry to the purists out there, but we go by the 'all things in moderation' mantra around here. Suffice it to say that few weeks go by in this household where the sprinkle stash doesn't make an appearance. Today, it made its appearance loud and proud.

Like many other days, today was a frozen-waffle-for-breakfast kind of day. To reiterate, waffles=sprinkles. Because I knew that it was a cleaning day and typically save the kitchen for last, I didn't put much effort into putting anything away before heading off on my conquest. Well, it wasn't terribly long after tending to tissues that I finished the bedrooms and headed downstairs to continue on. As I walked through the kitchen, I kicked something. A little plastic something. I looked down towards the floor and I discovered not one, not two, but three empty sprinkle containers. I shouted to Clark (because first-borns are blamed for everything…duh) and while he made his way to me, I assessed my surroundings.

Dozens of tiny, rainbow-colored spheres dotted the tiles of my kitchen floor. Prior to the toddler takeover, I knew that the bottles were each no more than a quarter full. Because of this, I didn't expect to see *gobs* of sprinkles underfoot, but I also knew that had they *all* been spilled or dumped...there would have been more remaining evidence. My guess? They were eaten. Clark arrived first on scene with typically colored lips, a mostly pink tongue, and no dead giveaways. Closely behind, however, followed a little girl who was not only caught red handed...she was caught pink and blue and purple and yellow handed AND faced, at that.

The fun doesn't end there, though. No, not just yet. When I proceeded to question Annie and say all of the necessary 'mom things' following a sprinkle snacking fest—things like *"We don't eat sprinkles without asking Mommy first"*—I was given new information:

"I didn't eat the sprinkles, Momma. I <u>spit</u> the sprinkles!"

In that moment, I don't even think I wanted to know what spitting sprinkles meant exactly. And what *did* it mean? Well, it meant that Annie put a whole lot of colorful sprinkles in her mouth for a period of time just long enough to turn them into a sticky, syrup-like heap of maroon-ish orbs and then proceeded to spit them for one reason or another onto my hardwood floor. Apparently the first oral evacuation wasn't enough, though, because I continued to find stray orbs here there and everywhere on the first floor all morning long. It was like an Easter egg hunt gone wrong[1].

I'd like to think that my toddlers did the things they did while I was cleaning today to spice up my efforts and pull me from the monotony of servanthood. We're going to go with that. Messes with toddlers? They're everywhere and they're never-ending. This is especially true when it comes to mealtime. As our 'tour' continues, I'd like you to join me in the room I am found most often: the kitchen.

Cooking is fairly simple, right? If we pare it down (I'm giggling at my sly food reference over here just in case you care…) it looks like this:

Prepare food. Eat food.

Before I had children, this was pretty much the case. The process was straightforward, I could eat what I wanted to when I wanted to, and the results of my culinary efforts were a benefit to *me*. When kids entered the scene, however, simple went out the window. Now, the process is no longer two-step. Today, it looks more like:

Prepare food. Cool food. Cut up food. Add ketchup (or sprinkles!) to food. Request that toddlers pause playtime for food. Demand that toddlers pause playtime for food. Carry toddlers from playtime to food. Serve food. Serve different food. Serve more food. Give permission to be done with food. Wipe faces and hands that are messy from food. Wipe tables and floors that are painted with food.

So much more effort goes into food preparation when toddlers are in the picture. Much like the endless feedings that are exhausting in the newborn days, keeping toddlers' bellies full is super-cyclical. You pour yourself into making a meal—most often receiving chastisement for getting *something* wrong—then pour yourself into cleaning up, are bombarded with requests for the next snack before cleanup is even finished, and at some point remember that you haven't eaten since breakfast. Food-related things are just a teensy bit more complicated with toddlers in the picture.

Keeping toddlers fed is constant service, and most of the time that service is ultra-thankless. One of my current beefs (I'm not even sure that you can use the word 'beef' that way, but I'm going to anyway) with serving toddlers in the realm of food is a habit that Clark has recently taken up. As soon as his plate hits the table, instead of a *"Thank you, Mommy!"* or an *"Mmmm, this looks good!"*, most of the time his food is greeted with the following: *"How many bites do I need to eat?"* Grrr. While this is especially maddening on nights when I've actually put forth effort into preparing a meal with my toddlers' tastes in mind, it would drive me nuts even if I slapped a Pop-Tart in front of him. Before tasting the food—heck, basically even before visualizing the food—my son is eager to know what is minimally required of him so that he can escape the prison that is our kitchen table. Being the sarcastic person I am, I've started responding to this heinous question with remarks like *"100"* or *"32"*. Let's just say they aren't well received. Touché, son. Soon enough, we will spend an entire chapter together in the world of 'food fun' when it comes to feeding felines. Until then, let's continue with our tour. Come on out to my garage with me.

Wherever they go, toddlers need entertainment. Be it Play-Doh, or markers, or puzzles with 1000's of pieces (OK…I guess most toddler versions only have like 30), these little minds are enriched and these little hands are engaged when activities are offered to keep them busy. At home, while entertainment in some form is offered *often*, it isn't always an absolute necessity. Without my intervention, there are plenty of things already in place for my toddlers to do. They can play with their toys, they can hide under brother's bunk bed fort, or they can use their imagination. In the car, though, entertainment is key.

When my children are free to move about and do as they please, they are much easier to placate. Restrain them in any way, shape, or form, however, and you'd better have a really good plan for distraction. If you've ever owned a cat who wanted no parts of being put in a pet carrier to go—well—*anywhere*, you know precisely what I mean. First, the cat spots the carrier and hides under the first bed it locates. Then, it digs its claws into the carpet and resists removal. Then, it scratches and fights and bites and makes itself rigid so that proper securement in the carrier is nearly impossible. And then, to make sure that the cat's disapproval is known, it continues to cry loudly alllllllll the way to wherever it's going.

If you are a toddler wrangler at present or have ever been one before, this process probably sounds familiar. Replace the cat in the illustration with Annie and the pet carrier with her car seat. This is my life. Being tethered or held down in any fashion goes against the inner workings of my toddlers. They are movers and shakers and being confined just doesn't jive well with them. Because of this, Jonathan and I have become unwilling cruise directors just about every time our four wheels leave the garage. We have to ensure that food, beverage, and activities are a'plenty…or else we have the wrath of unsatisfied and irate passengers to deal with.

Ever since my children were born, I have been nothing short of a servant on the road. If multitasking isn't your strength and you are in need of practice, try throwing three toddlers in the backseat of your car. It's pretty much trial by fire. Unless I am fully prepared and set each child up with something to eat, something to drink, and something to hold, driving anywhere involves a lot of demands and a lot of me trying my best to accurately toss distractions into stir-crazy laps[2]. Heck, even when I am fully prepared it's much the same. Pretty much every road trip is a flurry of demands strung less-than-gracefully together. Demands about windows. Demands about song choice. Demands about snotty noses, leaking cups, uncomfortable shoes, and glaring sunshine…all while I am trying my best to operate heavy machinery and ensure that all riders make it alive and in one piece from Point A to Point B.

Just recently, I had Annie, Clark, and Madison in tow on a particularly feisty day. I don't recall specifically why they were all in sour form—except being toddlers, of course—but both individually and collectively, they were much closer to salt than sugar on the sweetness scale. Everyone had about twenty complaints to voice, no one seemed to be much in the mood for a car ride, and I was pretty close to the end of my rope. Being the compassionate, empathetic, awesome mom that I am, I did the only thing I could think of in the moment. I BLARED the music loud, sang along, and pretended that I didn't have a couple of irate cats one and two rows behind me. They all responded in very typical, hilarious ways. Madison sucked her thumb in silence. Clark shouted at me and kicked the seat in front of him. And Annie? She cried real tears and said repeatedly, *"No one is talking to me. I don't have anyone to talk to."* You win some, you lose some.

It's all of these demands and all of this nonsense that leads parents of toddlers to put screens in front of faces and sugary substances in mouths. I so, so get it, and all too often I am in that place. Even this, however, adds to the chaos. Add in a screen, and suddenly there are dying batteries and crashing apps to deal with. Add in sugar, and it's gummies gone rogue and lollipops stuck in hair. Getting toddlers into the car is a battle in and of itself, but once they're there? It's survival of the fittest.

Whether it's inside of a messy house or the hostile environment of a vehicle, tending to toddlers is serving. It just is. It's putting so much time and effort into the care of others that you find yourself asking your spouse for 'permission' to use the bathroom, get dressed, or get a shower[3]. It's cleaning fermented urine and moldy apple remains from toy boxes (yup…happened). It's picking up dozens of tiny pieces of crayon wrapper each and every time coloring is offered yet offering it anyway. It's knowing the stains that dot every carpet and every piece of furniture in your home by name. It's constant laundry and constant dishes. It's peer mediation that never ends.

For these reasons and more, I channel Cinderella very often. She and I, we just get it. We get what it's like to prepare countless meals for thankless consumers. We get what it's like to clean up messes that reappear before they're even really gone. We get what it's like to hit the pillow on empty and wake to the killjoy that is the clock tower yet again. We get it.

This, however, is where my likeness to Cinderella ends. Unlike Cinderella, I have no birds or squirrels with which to sing cutesy tunes. Apart from dust bunnies, I am without rodent companions altogether under my roof. Further, I am lacking a Fairy Godmother. You know, the jovial, glowing, see-the-bright-side-of-everything assistant? The one with a magical wand capable of whisking away my problems and replacing the dirt on my face with deftly applied makeup? No, I don't have one of those[4]. What I *do* have, however, is perspective. Specifically, I have what I dub 'the 5 AM perspective'.

We've already established that I don't do mornings. I value sleep, I love sleep, and I hold onto it way too tightly. What I have come to realize, though, is that nothing is as bad as it inherently seems if I own it. So, while 5 AM is ugly, awful, and simply not a time of day that my eyes should witness *independently*, 5 AM isn't so terrible if I shift my focus. If I focus on all of the sleep I have lost since I became a mom, or focus on the number of days I have slept until 8 AM or later in the last four and a half years (that would be like a whopping two), or focus on the very-long list of servants' tasks that await me most days…it makes me mopey. If I focus instead on all of the things I have gained since I became a mom, or focus on the things I give back to myself by rising early, or focus on the reality that I don't 'have to' do any of these tasks but 'get to'…it makes me joyful. Yes, really.

I *get to* be the first face that sees my children in the morning. I *get to* choose how their bodies are nourished and their minds are enriched every day. I *get to* be the one to do preschool drop-offs. Even on days when all that it seems I 'get to' do is clean and cook and correct, I know that I am still privileged with a gift that many others wish for, and I am thankful. Along with their cute-bottomed Daddy, my children are the very best part of my life and I would trade all of the sleep in the world and—brace yourselves—even all of the coffee in the world to keep them safe, loved, and provided for. Bring it on, 5 AM. I see you, I'm ready for you, and I'll continue to best you day in and day out.

Parenting toddlers isn't about how many times you fall into the muck that comes along with servanthood. It's about how long you allow yourself to wallow there. It's about rising up, rocking your muddy attire, and serving your children even when serving is hard. They need your service. They benefit from your service. They grow from your service. Being a servant isn't always fun and isn't always immediately gratifying, but it certainly *is* rewarding in a larger sense. Around here, we've got messes upon messes upon messes…but we've got progress too. Occasionally, we have peaceful car rides. Occasionally, we have dinners that come with *"Mommy, this is the best meal ever!"* Occasionally, we have crayon marks that make it onto a piece of paper turned into a just-because 'card' for Daddy instead of on the walls. Each and every day, I see little glimpses of progress. Some days those glimpses are teeny-teeny-tiny, but they're there. And so, I'll keep serving. Speaking of which…I've got dishes to unload, dinner to prep, and Clark's rest-time clock is about to alarm. Until tomorrow, guys!

Footnotes

[1] As I sit down to edit this, it's now been two days since our sprinkle 'celebration'. In case you are wondering…I'm still finding them.

[2] Funny/not funny story. Once, I nailed Clark in the face with his aluminum cup.

[3] Usually in front of an audience, no less.

[4] I better be nominated Wife of the Year over here for this one (kidding!), but I do have to take a little timeout at this point to acknowledge that while I may not have a Fairy Godmother, I do indeed have a Prince Charming. In the lottery of husbands, I hit the jackpot and have been gifted with a spouse who sort of does whisk away my problems at the end of the day. He supports me always, loves me unconditionally, and is an A++++ father. He is a super-decent human being who shares fully in the work of raising our children, and I am very thankful that none of the experiences I write about in this book—good or bad—are encountered alone. For the cat herders out there who are reading this and are either a Cinderella without a Prince or a Prince without a Cinderella, you are rock stars. You have my respect and deserve recognition. What you do every day on your own is hard, hard stuff.

4 ANTICS IN PERSONAL HYGIENE

If you're a savvy reader, you may be wondering how it is possible that I spent an entire chapter on serving toddlers yet never touched on the effort it takes to keep them clean and semi-presentable to the public. You know, hair that isn't matted. Clothing that isn't tackier than glue given the amount of jelly it's coated in. Teeth that aren't still holding tight to dinner from last Tuesday. Skin that is actually sun-kissed and not just bronzed with mud. That kind of presentable. Well, reader, this is because you and I are about to go there. Big time. My children despise any and everything that relates to hygiene. They seriously do. Bathing, dressing, and grooming of all sorts are sure-fire ways to take my kids from blissful to ballistic in the blink of an eye. They aren't fans.

In some ways, this is kind of entertaining as it provides for loads of laugh-worthy stories—a few of which I promise to share shortly—but mostly it's just infuriating. In the world of parenting, Jonathan and I each have a tipping point. That tipping point varies from day to day based on other stressors like fatigue (both of us), workload (Jonathan), and hormones (me!)...but I can say with 122% certainty that matters of hygiene take the cake for both of us on tipping point triggers. It's really, really, really difficult to be even-keeled with our toddlers when we hit hygiene-related speed bumps again and again and again.

If I could have a penny for all of the times I've heard *"I don't want to take a bath!"* or *"I don't want to get dressed!"* or *"I don't want to brush my teeth!"* since I earned the title of Mom, I would be sitting pretty on a mountain of copper by now. I'd be swimming in those pennies, making penny angels, donating pennies to the lost causes of the world, and using those pennies to buy gourmet popcorn and ice cream by the boatload. On the other hand, however, if I had to *contribute* a penny to the Swear Jar—or Lost It Jar in my case—for all of the times that hygienic conundrums have taken me over the ledge? Well, I guess we're even-stevens. Bye bye pennies!

For as much as my children love to splash in water and make a total mess of our bathroom once they make it to the tub, they put up one heck of a fight to get in it. Every. Single. Time. I guess it's just their deep-seated kitty quirks shining through…but bath time absolutely baffles me. If and when either Clark or Annie catch wind that bath time is nearing, they protest. They whine. They grumble. They stomp their little feet. Until it actually happens, bath time is always perceived as pure torture and the very worst idea in the world.

About 95% of the time, as soon as their toes touch down in the tub, though, bath time takes a 180 from punishment to play. On these occasions, Jonathan and I get to be 'meanies' twice. We have to basically chase down our children and force them into the bath, and then—typically for reasons such as running out of hot water, a looming bedtime, or skin that is shriveled beyond its recognizable form[1]—we have to force those same children out of the tub. Play time baths require a variety of forms of entertainment including water coloring tabs, soap markers, bowls, shovels, cars, 108 wash cloths, a 'shaving kit' (thanks, Spahrs!), and sometimes even extraneous objects such as rocks (who knows). All too often, the kids' bath tub is one part trash can, one part toy box, and one part art project.

And then, unlike the long-yet-pleasant play time baths, there are the forced variety. Thankfully, these baths only make up about 5% of our total experiences over here, but they're anxiety-producing even to think about. Be it for reasons of exhaustion or hunger or just toddlers being toddlers, there are occasional times where the protests don't end when toes meet tub. Instead, they get louder, more violent, and persist until (and much after, actually) the bath is over. Forced baths are no fun. Forced baths are frustrating. *Frustrating*-frustrating. Raging toddlers in their typical forms are already difficult enough to deal with, but add in soap that stings eyes and water that makes skin ridiculously slippery? Awesome.

I think a fun/gross experiment would be to let Clark and Annie go as long as they wanted to without a bath before they actually arrived at a point of suggesting it themselves. I'm pretty certain they'd start growing mold before this ever came to be and that I'd be arrested, however, so I guess we'll stick with what we know. Pee in the tub always. More water on the bather than the bathe-ee. A bathroom floor that winds up drenched. Bumps and bruises resulting from ignored warnings that jumping in the tub is not a good idea. Blue soap on the ceiling (how on Earth, guys?). Endless questions and comments about body parts. *This* is the stuff we know when it comes to bath time.

And then, there's the beast known as dressing. If I allowed it, my children would live in their pajamas for all of time. I know, I know…who wouldn't, right? But for real, this is another battle I fight every single day of my life. Clark doesn't like the idea of getting dressed as a whole. He doesn't like what it means and what it stands for. You see, Clark is just like me in that he is an introvert who benefits greatly from fresh air. It's an interesting dichotomy and a constant struggle. Like me, Clark loves the comfort, protection and familiar environment of his own abode, yet he gets stir crazy quickly and thrives when he can expend his energy beyond the walls of his home…especially in outdoor settings. For me, it's kind of like this:

Give me ALL the sunshine and ALL the fresh air, but only make me get out of bed on my own terms. Oh, and human interaction? I'm going to have to call the shots on that one too.

When we are stressed or overstimulated, Clark and I both need the retreat that our own audience-free home offers. So why does Clark hate getting dressed? He hates getting dressed because he knows it most likely means we're leaving that safety net. If he feels that he has control over the situation, knows that leaving is of benefit to him, or is just going somewhere he really, really wants to go (typically to Lowe's or for froyo…smart kid), getting him dressed is slightly less of a workout. Slightly.

Unlike Clark, Annie's contempt for dressing has nothing to do with going or not going anywhere. Annie hates getting dressed simply because she doesn't want to stop moving. Remember how we talked about the car seat and any form of restraint? In Annie's world, having to halt her own goings-on for even 30 seconds is abuse. Trying to get Annie dressed is like trying to put a pair of pants on an octopus. Two holes, eight legs. Not going to happen.

I have tried all forms of options when it comes to dressing. I've tried letting my toddlers choose their own outfits, and I've tried doing the choosing for them. I've tried dressing them way before it's absolutely necessary, and I've tried waiting until the last possible moment. I've tried setting outfits out the night before. I've tried letting them dress themselves. I've tried bribery. I've tried threats. My kids just despise getting dressed.

So we've established that if it were up to them, my children would be smelly nudists…but that's only the start. They'd be smelly nudists…with dreadlocks. Annie would have dreads because she flees at the sight of a comb or hairbrush and wants no involvement in taming the tresses she inherited directly from her mommy: straight on the top, curly underneath. Clark, on the other hand, would have dreads because he loathes haircuts. Before we jump into the world of present-day haircuts, let's journey back in time to Clark's very first experience with lopping locks.

As an 18-month-old, Clark was busy, busy, busy and prone to shifts in mood. Not much has changed. Because his sister's arrival was only a few months away, Jonathan and I decided to plan a trip to Disney World for our final getaway as a family of three. When we discovered that first haircuts at Magic Kingdom were not only super-cheap by Disney standards but included mouse ears and a flipping certificate…we were sold. In pure Disney style, a first haircut at Magic Kingdom is a song and dance and something to be remembered. We booked this experience well in advance which gave us lots of time to envision how things would likely go. All of our best guesses included screaming, kicking, and bloodshed on Clark's part, and sweat, frustration, and a big old tip on the part of the barber. Luckily for us, we were wrong.

Clark's first haircut was a dream. He proved Jonathan and me wrong in every way and sort of had us speechless. Our never-still, often hostile toddler sat with a smile on his face and a light-up toy in his hand the entire time. We have it on video as proof. It was a precious and priceless 'first' that I'll never forget. All of the haircuts since this one, however? Well, I wouldn't be quite so sad to forget those.

Haircuts with Clark today are hilariously awful. In the moment they're more awful than hilarious, but in hindsight they're absolutely laughable. Haircuts cause my son such great anxiety that I have to give him at least three days' notice and even still, he *begs* me to let the idea pass. During a haircut, Clark contorts, cringes, and cries. No matter the bribery—be it his favorite show or a hair-covered lollipop—and no matter the comfort measures taken—like powder to the neck or even plastic wrap taped below the hair line (yes, we've tried it)—Clark just can't stand the process. The predominant reason for his ridiculousness is that *I* have assumed the role of barber. No longer does Clark have a perky, friendly, calmer-than-calm cast member behind the buzzer. He's got a much less friendly, let's-get-this-over-with mom to deal with. I am certain that Clark would behave in a completely different fashion if someone else was cutting his hair. Why, then, you ask do I put myself and Clark through the misery? Three words. I am cheap.

If I have the ability to cut Clark's hair and save our family a few dollars every other month, it's going to happen. Saving money where we can so that we can spend money where we want to is just what Jonathan and I do. It's why I also give Jonathan haircuts, why I haven't had my own hair professionally cut or colored in *years*, why I am known for wearing underwear that are falling apart, why our house just might always have seashell sinks from the 80's, why the majority of our children's toys and clothing have made their way through about ten other kiddos before they land in our laps, and why Jonathan powers himself through wheel bearing replacements and gas line installation (pray for us...ha!) with the help of YouTube. It's spending less in these areas that are of minimal importance to us that allows us to spend more in those that we would rather not live without: good food and good fun.

Apart from select people, of course, there is little that I love more on planet Earth than well-made food. Jonathan can attest to this, but I told him long ago to forget the jewelry and the flowers. A pint of quality ice cream or a giant soft pretzel speaks love to me far louder. In the realm of saving money when it comes to food, shopping at Aldi[2] on the whole where I can spend a mere 59 cents on a pound of pretzels for my snack-inhaling children allows me to justify the purchase of jars of peanut butter elsewhere that cost over $10 without an ounce of regret[3].

As far as 'good fun', Jonathan and I execute a similar balance of saving and splurging. Most of the time, we seek out free or minimally expensive fun for our family when it comes to outings and adventures. More often than not, you can find us exploring at a local park, playing at a York County library, noshing on samples at a nearby market, or participating in a free fest of some sort. Finding fun without significant expense the majority of the time is what allows us to spend more freely on vacations and day trips. Far more than we are 'stuff' people, we are 'memories' and 'experiences' people, and we want Clark and Annie to see, and take in, and taste it all. The bottom line when it comes to our family is this: Save where we can. Splurge where we want. This is all, of course, within reason...but you get the basic gist.

Spending money in and of itself weighs heavily on me as a cheapskate, but I especially don't like spending money in areas that aren't fun or personally beneficial. This isn't a novel concept and is probably something that most people can relate to. Paying bills kind of stinks, but electricity, water, and trash collection are all things that I directly benefit from. Because of this, I suck it up, put on my adult pants, and (let my husband) submit our dues. You know what is neither fun nor beneficial to me, though? The costs associated with the root canals that my children are going to someday need. Big surprise, but Clark and Annie aren't fans of oral hygiene either.

Just like all other things, my toddlers prefer when brushing their teeth happens on their own watch and by their own submission. If Jonathan or I tell Annie that it's time to brush her teeth, she is the furthest thing from a willing participant. She is the same child, however, that I find covered in toothpaste at least three times a day. Painting with toothpaste and eating toothpaste are acceptable in Annie's world, apparently, but brushing teeth with it just isn't fun or rewarding enough.

With Clark, it's mostly just that Jonathan and I never quite get toothbrushing *right* by his standards. If we top his toothbrush with bubblegum-flavored paste, he wants mint. If we go in the mint direction, he finds it appalling. Should we come at him with his favorite, pink brush...well of course he wants the green one he got at preschool. But if we choose that one from the start? It's:

"Mommmmmmmmy. I told you, the <u>pink</u> one is my favorite."

Clark's behavior during toothbrushing at home is especially ironic considering how saintly he is in a dentist's chair. When it's a stranger working on his mouth, Clark sits unmoving, follows instructions, and allows basically anything to take place. The very first time that Clark saw our dentist, Jonathan and I were forewarned that he had deep pits in his baby molars which would likely result in cavities no matter the effort we put forth in brushing. Unfortunately, this warning was completely accurate, and a cavity was discovered shortly after Clark's fourth birthday.

Because the cavity was deep and a good bit of drilling was required, a numbing shot was needed. Clark could have cared less. He sat like a statue while a topical cream took effect, didn't even flinch when a needle came at him, and was a happy camper from start to finish. Daddy had taken him to the appointment that day, and Clark came home amped to tell me all about the dental equipment he got to see. I will say that we have a pretty cool dentist who is wonderful with young patients (thanks, Dr. Green!), but I think my toddlers simply prefer saving their worst behavior for Jonathan and me. It's the hair cutting thing all over again. If a barber cuts it, Clark's an angel. If I do it, he's quite the opposite. While I am super-not complaining about this as I wouldn't want my children out in the world acting like complete jerks for strangers, I will just say…it's *so* frustrating to know what they're capable of.

In the world of hygiene hatred, there is one more principal self-care necessity that puts my toddlers up in arms. As I unveil and unpack this final facet of our discussion, I'll be honest in saying that as compared to bathing, dressing, haircare and oral care, this is typically the area that Clark and Annie put up the least amount of fight for. They still avoid it and try to barter their way out of it, don't get me wrong, but it's simply a lesser offender than the others. What am I referring to? Nail trimming.

Without parental intervention, Clark and Annie would look a lot like Edward Scissorhands. Their nails could be inches long and harboring all sorts of dirt, food, and craft time remnants, and I'm pretty sure they'd never take notice. I love it when my own children best illustrate the point I am discussing, but in this case I'm going to tap into the niece and nephew pool for a beyond-ludicrous and VERY hilarious depiction of nail care toddler style. My kids have hidden in toy boxes and behind couches to avoid the nail clippers, but it's Tristan again who takes the cake on this one[4].

As a toddler, Tristan went beyond hating having his toenails trimmed. I don't even think there's an appropriate word, in fact, for exactly how he felt about it. Kind of like Clark despises haircuts and dives straight into banshee mode when the buzzer comes out of the closet, Tristan used to go full-on demon possession when Alicia or Joe had to trim his nails. The kid acted like he was being killed. Actually, he *wanted* to be killed. I'm not even joking. As a four-year-old toddler, Tristan would pray, out loud, for Jesus to let him die. As if this story isn't complete or colorful enough, it goes even further, however. To avoid the morbid pleas, Alicia and Joe discovered that allowing Tristan to bite down on a sock, of all things, helped to keep him somewhat silent and much less agitated. Tristan essentially had to be bound and gagged…to get his *nails trimmed*. Ha. Ha. Ha. At the time it was a bit disturbing if I'm being frank, but now it just makes for yet another thing for my sisters and me to laugh about and reminisce upon. We have SO much material with which to embarrass our children in the future. It's going to be all kinds of awesome.

Just like many cats have less-than-affectionate feelings towards being brushed, bathed, and short-clawed, my toddlers and many toddlers of the world have animosity towards grooming. This animosity, in turn, results in requiring even more effort of parents who are already exhausted and taxed well beyond their capacity day in and day out. Let's get real for a second. Who really *wants* to give their child a bath or *wants* to comb through their tangled hair? While these things are absolutely necessary and are things we do willingly and with love and an attitude of (here it comes again…) <u>service</u> as parents, they aren't things we choose to do for fun. Add an unwilling and unhappy toddler on top of a task that isn't something you're super looking forward to to begin with? It's a real struggle. The reality and the hope, however, is that there's redemption even in hygiene hatred if you look closely enough for it.

For starters, if there ever comes a day in cat herding where you or I throw up our hands in surrender and wave the white flag to the little people who are begging that bath time wait until tomorrow, I say this: *The sun will still rise if a bath is missed or intentionally avoided.* Every single day, I pick my battles, and you know what? Some days the hygienic type aren't worth fighting. You can bet your boots that my kids have been found traipsing around in the same outfit for a solid 48 hours or more. Like way-more, more. Have there been days without a single good toothbrushing? Oh yeah. Evenings where neither Jonathan nor I can muster the energy to give a way overdue bath. Mmm-hmm. Believe it or not, even on these days the world carries on, my children survive, and I still consider myself a decent mom.

On the tougher days, however, the days when surrendering is not an option and when the decisions you make for your children's wellbeing are not well received…take heart. There are learning opportunities for your little ones, and there are learning opportunities for you as a parent too. When Jonathan and I decide for Clark and Annie that hygiene is not optional, we are showing them that while their preferences are known and heard, sometimes they are simply overridden when it comes to matters of welfare. Setting expectations and standards for hygiene demonstrates to them that taking care of themselves, although not always fun, has to be a priority. As my children grow, I hope they come to learn and recognize the reality that they've only got one body and one shot at life with which to take care of that body. Maybe it's a stretch, but I'd like to believe that sometimes putting my foot down when it comes to bath time or brushing teeth or getting dressed shows that I stand for doing what's best, not what's easiest. My hope is that these simple, second nature things like brushing hair and bathing will roll over into bigger, more intentional things like exercising and eating healthy in the future. I can hope, right?

Have you ever been in one of those stressful situations during which if you don't laugh the stress away, you might cry? Well that was me only a handful of days back. I was downstairs trying my best to manage a maniacal Clark during his much-needed haircut while Jonathan was upstairs tending to a maniacal Annie during her much-needed scrub in the tub. I couldn't do anything but laugh. If you happen to find yourself in my neighborhood on a warm, spring day—a windows open kind of day—and are suddenly enveloped by the sounds of screaming as you walk past my home, I hope you'll laugh too. It must be bath time!

Footnotes

[1] Here's some useless, yet fun, trivia for you. Did you know that wrinkly skin during bath time is believed to be a tool to enhance grip? For years, apparently, scientists thought that this reaction was simply the skin's response to being waterlogged, but they now propose that it's actually an intentional process. Like tires needing tread to grip wet surfaces, wet feet require wrinkles to keep a person upright and wet hands require wrinkles to be able to pick up objects. Weird, right?

[2] Frugality runs in my family, and the very best example of this is my sister Ashley. It was Ashley who introduced me to the wonders of Aldi. It's my favorite grocery store ever. About a decade back, Ashley wanted desperately to be a stay at home mom even though it wasn't exactly a financial option. To make it happen, she started an in-home daycare and did ANYthing to save a buck. You know those little yogurt smoothies that kids love? The ones that feature a monkey on the packaging? She made her own. She hoarded empty containers from the neighbors, bought cheap yogurt in bulk, mixed it with milk, and poured it back into the bottles. Today, financial strain is no longer a hurdle for Ashley and Kyle. I witnessed with my own eyes a 38-pack of store-bought monkey yogurts (gasp!) at their son's birthday party this past weekend. Old habits die hard, though, I suppose because I also witnessed Ashley cooking chicken nuggets on a stone sheet pan that had lost about a third of its original mass from being dropped on the floor and listened to her tell stories of her old jalopy of a minivan. When the heater died on her minivan last week, Ashley's response was: "I'll just have the boys use blankets if we have any more cold spring mornings!" Oh, how I love you sissy.

[3] I'm eating a spoonful of said peanut butter as I type this, in fact, and it's delicious. Right this very second, grab your credit card and hop on over to www.blindspotnutbutters.com. Your life will be better. My spoon currently contains a seasonal flavor, Peanut Butter Marshmallow Dream, and it is easily one of the best things I have ever put in my mouth. Am I right or am I right, Meg?

[4] Sorry bud, but you're quite a star in this book. Be forewarned that this isn't the last time you'll appear, either. For the record, I told your mom that I'd ask your permission if she wanted me to and received the following: "He's still a minor. He has no say." Ha!

5 NEVER-EVER-EVER-ENDING ILLNESS

You know those little rubber balls that bounce around like crazy? The ones you can grab from a quarter machine in just about any grocery store? Those suckers are all over the place in a flash and once they're on the move, they can be quite difficult to catch. Essentially, those bouncy balls are my toddlers. My children are intense and they are active and they have more energy packed inside of a single hair on their heads than I think I have ever, ever possessed. If it wasn't for Jonathan and me rounding them up for rest time in the afternoon or bedtime in the evening, I'm pretty sure they would just go and go and go. I'm also pretty sure that whatever is pumping through their veins could be the antidote to tranquilizer. *Elephant* tranquilizer. I love to see my children's vitality and vigor in action. I love to see how they take in and take on the world. I love that they love adventure and exploration and everything the opposite of being couch potatoes. I love it all…but the truth is it's exhausting to watch let alone manage.

All of what I have just spoken about my children has been a rather long-winded way of getting around to the focus of this chapter: illness. I realize that I may have lost you and that you might be wondering how exactly my children's inclination towards action and movement relates to sickness, but believe me…there's a link. You see, every once in a while one or both of my toddlers presents in a fashion quite unlike the norm. Every once in a while, they are calm, quiet, cooperative and subdued. I'm talking about a rare day in which Clark or Annie actually listens to me, stays in one place for longer than five whole seconds, or doesn't have four million things to say. While it would be nice if these sorts of days simply came as a change of pace and as a beacon of hope that even the challenges of toddlerhood are temporary…that is not why they come around here. Almost always without fail, a calm Bausman is a sick Bausman.

Generally speaking, toddlerhood is a stage of life that is filled with snot and vomit. Toddlers are germy little beings who adore putting everything in their mouths from their own hands, to the contents of their nasal passages, to the bottoms of dirty shoes. Often times, toddlerhood is a game of hopscotch on repeat. These tots simply jump from one illness to the next to the next. Sometimes, in all reality, it feels like toddlers are sick more often than they are healthy.

Before I dive deep into the world of toddler yuck, I would like to take a moment to acknowledge something very important. Although my children have been sick or snotty more times than I can count in their short, little lives, I am fully aware of and extraordinarily grateful for the fact that neither of them has ever been seriously or chronically ill. If you are reading this chapter and are not able to say the same for your own child(ren), please know how sincerely sorry I am. Children are meant to laugh, to explore the world, and to get messy. When illness limits these things, it takes a heavy toll not only on the affected child but on all of those around him or her. While I may make light of my own experiences with 'sick' children and look at this facet of my current life with humor in the pages to come, please know that I know how very *not* funny illness can be.

Because of sickness, having toddlers means constantly juggling, rearranging, and canceling events, get-togethers, and even workdays. This is exaggerated to the Nth degree when you also have friends who have toddlers. Allow me to demonstrate. Jonathan and I are fortunate enough to journey together on the ride of parenthood and live within about two minutes of close friends of ours, Matt and

Sabrina. We all graduated from the same college, have worked together in different capacities over the past 15 or so years, and have just always jived well as a group.

Matt and Sabrina welcomed their first little one, Lillie Jane, to the world only weeks before Jonathan and I welcomed Clark. In those first months as moms, Sabrina and I sort of became a life-line for one another. We started sending pages-long messages back and forth with support, humor, advice, and commiseration. Throughout the years, our messages have gotten shorter as much of parenting has become old hat, but we continue to check in frequently and try to get our clan, which now includes Annie and Roslynn, together once a month.

Today is March 29. Take a stab at when we got together last. September 22. I'm not even kidding. While Jonathan and I have been together with portions of the Pannucci family sporadically over the past six months (Jonathan once with Matt, and me once with Sabrina and the girls), more than half of an entire year has passed since we've pulled off a play-date with all parties present. Since September, Sabrina and I have made at least a half-dozen attempts at joining our families. Time and time and time again, however, toddler crud has reigned victorious over our efforts. In February, the poor Pannuccis bounced from colds, to fevers, to stomach viruses, to pink eye all within a matter of about a week. In case we never see you again, Pannuccis, it's been real.

We have gone months without seeing our friends because of the illnesses of four tiny humans. In the world of toddlers, there really and truly are seasons of nothing but sick. Why is it that these guys always seem to have a faucet for a nose, a cough that puts a smoker to shame, or a forehead fevered enough to fry eggs? Well, because they are gross. Capital G Gross, mind you. Jonathan and I used to roll our eyes when we had doctor's visits for Clark and they would ask us all of those mandatory lead paint questions. Questions like *"does your child live in or regularly visit a home that was built before 1978?"* I remember one time specifically being asked this question when Clark was immobile and only a few months old. Jonathan and I were together at the appointment and we answered honestly and politely, but when the nurse exited the room we had a conversation like this:

> JONATHAN: I always feel like those lead paint questions are stupid.

> ME: I know. Why would it even matter if Clark was around lead paint, it's not like he's going to be licking the walls or eating paint chips as snacks.

Oh, naive Whitney. How very little you knew.

As it turns out, toddlers do lick walls. Fast forward a year from the doctor's office conversation above. Jonathan's father, an expert-level painter, had just finished painting Annie's nursery. It's important to know that when my father-in-law does something, he does it right. This, in turn, meant that not only were Annie's walls painted, but her ceiling, trim work, and window sill were too. Only minutes after Dad had wrapped up the project and left us with dry, but still tacky, paint, Clark proceeded to hoist himself up onto Annie's window and drag his teeth along the sill much like a beaver. It was a full circle moment. Toddlers very much *do* eat paint, I promise. The next time you're asked silly questions at the pediatrician's office, parents, don't snicker. Clark can thank his lucky stars that we don't have lead-based paint around here.

Since they became mobile, my children have been licking and ingesting disgusting things right and left. It doesn't stop at paint, though. You see...in my house, toddlers lick floors and trash cans too. Whether or not it is a direct result of the things my children insist on tasting—like the entire length of a Target cart the day before leaving for vacation (repulsive, Annie)—the toddler years have certainly been germ-filled years for us. In order to best reflect on the variety of microbes that have invaded our home, our bodies, and our immune systems, I am going to break down this discussion into the following categories: coughs, barfs, fevers, and random crummies. There's no time like the present, I suppose…away we go!

Coughs

Along with drippy noses, coughing has got to be the symptom of illness that my toddlers and the majority of the toddlers exhibit most often. Coughs are annoying and bothersome at any age, really, but they're especially frustrating in the realm of toddlers because, one: there isn't much that can be done in the way of treatment and, two: they last for freaking ever. Apart from warm fluids, honey, and the humidifier[1] as comfort measures, coughs simply have to run their course in most cases. It would be nice if this happened in like a day or even a more-than-generous week as is the norm with most other symptoms but oh, no. Coughs just love to settle into little lungs for weeks on end and keep mommies and daddies cooped up indoors where they are led to stir-craziness and the brink of all-out breakdowns.

It is this stir-craziness that leads parents to cave and take their no longer contagious but still super yucky sounding children out into the public where lots of judgy eyes cast evil glances. Like the time I was out with Clark at the grocery store a solid two weeks into a cough. I was speed shopping like there was no tomorrow because I knew that it was only a matter of time before he coughed on something or someone…and that someone ended up being the disapproving lady behind me in line as I bent down away from the cart to grab a few paper bags at checkout. Sorry, lady! I promise anything he had wasn't catching by that point, my cabinets and refrigerator were barren, and my husband was starting to ask when dinner would involve an appliance apart from the toaster. Normally, when you're in between illnesses and have healthy toddlers in tow, hearing another child on the playground cough makes you cringe a little. But when your child is three weeks deep in her own yuck and you're desperate for a little fresh air…that same sound weirdly gives you relief. It's like an "*I feel you*", fraternity-building kind of experience.

In our home, coughs are more of a problem for Annie than they are for her brother. Clark has had his fair share of coughing through the years and is pretty typical in the department of colds, but Annie simply gets clobbered every time. As soon as Annie develops a runny nose or the mildest of a cold, a barking, awful-sounding cough is right around the corner. According to her pediatrician, Annie simply has narrow upper airways and will eventually "grow out of" this sort of response to respiratory illness, but right now it's very stressful and sometimes even downright scary. Coughs with Annie mean using all of the homeopathic basics along with steam treatments, the occasional use of a nebulizer, and even a steroid from time to time. Coughs with Annie mean lots of lost sleep on the part of our poor girl along with Jonathan and me. Coughs with Annie mean sometimes watching her struggle just to exchange air and aching, hurting hearts for a mommy and daddy who want nothing more for their little one than rest and comfort. Coughs suck.

Barfs

If you're a squeamish reader, this section might be a good one to skip. You've been warned. If you're sticking with me…here's a joke for you as a pity payment for all of the carnage you're about to be subjected to.

Why did the cannibal vomit after his meal? …….
I guess you really can't keep a good man down.

Sorry! It maybe made me roll my eyes too, but only after I giggled a little bit.

Anyway, while the cats I call toddlers may not leave me gifts in the form of hairballs on my carpet…believe me when I say that they make hairballs enviable. Oh, the joys of toddler vomit. It's violent, it's volatile, it's unpredictable, and it's EVERYWHERE. In the past three and a half years, I have had toddler barf on my clothes, on my brand new carpet, on my couch, in my car[2], in my hair, in my hands, and—sure did—in my mouth. Fun stuff. I'll never forget the very first time either of my two came down with a case of the belly bug. Unluckily for me, Jonathan had just left for a work conference in Vegas when I got the dreaded SOS call from Ashley.

ME: Hey, what's up? Is everything OK?

ASH: Well, I think so. Clark hasn't napped for me today and he's up in the pack 'n play crying pretty loud. I didn't know if you wanted me to just forget about nap and grab him, or if I should make him cry it out and see if he falls asleep eventually.

ME: Hmmm... ok, well—

ASH: Oh! Oh never mind. I can see it on the monitor. He blew. There's barf everywhere.

ME: Crap! Oh no, poor bud. I'll be there ASAP.

And off I flew (driving exactly the speed limit, of course) to gather up my poor little barf ball. Upon arrival, I scooped him up and loved on every vomit-covered ounce of him, fastened him inside of his car seat, and then proceeded to catch the next round of crud in my unprepared, bare hands. It was a 'fun' 15 minute ride home. If I remember correctly, I think Clark was sick another two times, and I, as an inexperienced newbie at all of this, was worried and stressing big time.

Since that first Christening, Jonathan and I have encountered and overcome many rounds of belly distress with our toddlers. You could say we're puking pros. We've called the nurse triage line at our pediatrician's office so many times over the years for vomit-related questions and concerns that I honestly think we could recite the protocol for stomach-sick toddlers verbatim. We even stock electrolyte replacement drinks and crackers in our pantry at all times. Some folks prepare for the apocalypse. We prepare for the barfs.

Unlike adults who, for the most part, can sense a problem in the belly region and get where they need to get before there's a mess and breakfast is revisited, toddlers can't. When Clark or Annie get sick this way, it is the furthest thing from controlled or foreseen. In a matter of mere seconds, my toddlers can go from chugging chocolate milk to 'tossing their cookies'. Because of this, there are a plethora of objects in my home that have been unsuspectingly doused in stomach contents.

This unpredictable, Jekyll and Hyde-like polarity is especially evident in Annie as a two-year-old...but even as an older toddler who can semi-express discomfort and anticipate that something is happening in the GI region, Clark remains anything but 'neat' or 'accurate' when it comes to barfing in a bucket. Understandably so, Clark has grown to resent the dreaded bucket and knows that it only makes an appearance when unpleasant hours lie ahead. For this reason, he *fights* the bucket and makes statements such as "*I don't want to be sick*" or "*I'm not going to be sick*"...even as it's happening. There's simply no rationalizing with a toddler who doesn't understand sickness and who would rather be experiencing just about anything else.

The most notable example of a toddler's lack of rational thinking when it comes to the barfs pertains to food. Simultaneously being hungry and stomach sick is a weird dynamic even for older children and adults. Our guts long for nourishment, but because we understand and accept that providing such sustenance is only going to end in further anguish and demise, we abstain a little longer. In the world of a toddler, however, being hungry is never something to be ignored. I couldn't even fathom a guess at the number of times either Clark or Annie has outright begged Jonathan and me for food or drink immediately after vomiting. When all we are able to offer are sips of clear liquids or nibbles of bland carbs here and there, it really does pain our hearts as parents to deprive our sick and non-discerning children…especially when they're looking at us with those sad, tear-filled eyes. My favorite-favorite, that's-my-daughter example of this? When Annie was *begging* for donuts mere seconds after being sick for the umpteenth time: "*I want dooooooooonuts. I want dooooooooooonuts.*" Who doesn't? Barfs suck.

Fevers

The uncharacteristic stillness I spoke of at the beginning of this chapter is almost always associated with fevers among my two. Fevers are kind of like their kryptonite. Not much else on planet Earth takes or keeps Clark and Annie down, but holy cow can a fever ever do the job. Much like the belly bug shows its face unexpectedly and leaves my floor covered in vomit, fevers tend to take Clark and Annie from playing to plastered on the couch in no time flat.

Even as a nurse, fevers have scared me on a few occasions because they have the ability to spike so quickly. More than once, a quieter-than-usual Annie has gone from warm to blazing in mere moments. While this has resulted in some hilarious things—even more hilarious than usual, I might add—escaping her lips due to fever-induced delirium[3], it is a tense and precarious experience that I much prefer to avoid.

As compared to other symptoms, there is one minutely 'good' thing about fevers amongst toddlers, which is that they are treatable in and of themselves with medication. When a fever is the result of a basic virus which is most often the case, a simple dose of ibuprofen or acetaminophen is typically all it takes to get my kiddos perked up and bouncing again. Because of this, there are times when fevers can be super short-lived and inconsequential. This is a good news/bad news situation, however. Have you ever tried giving an uncooperative cat medication? If you have, you feel me already. If you haven't, it's the exact opposite of fun.

I used to have an asthmatic cat who required oral steroids on a daily basis. I fully believe that this cat was the universe's way of preparing me for parenting toddlers. He was prone to grumpiness, he was cooperative only on his own terms, and he ran away from me basically any time I needed to do something other than give him a treat. Sound familiar? Getting this cat to take pills was an exhausting chore. I tried just about every song and dance I could come up with to get a teeny-tiny pill properly situated in his stomach—a pill to keep him breathing, nonetheless—and ultimately resorted to the barbaric method of 'shove and shut'. Shove the pill down the throat and hold the jaws shut.

While medicating toddlers may be a smidge more gentle, sometimes, it's pretty darn close to feline form. Annie, especially, is not a medicine kind of gal, tells us it's 'yucky', and proceeds to decline pharmaceutical relief. Most of the time she wears far more than she consumes, and our counters and floors are left in sticky, grape-scented shambles. You know what you do with toddlers whose fevers are 103 and don't cooperate in taking medicine? Acetaminophen suppositories. Let's just say that Annie is equally displeased with medication regardless of how it enters her bloodstream. Fevers suck.

Random Crummies

While coughs, barfs, and fevers are the most common symptoms of illness that my children exhibit, there are lots of others that cannot be so neatly categorized. Hence, I dub all that remains the random crummies. Random crummies include the pink eye that both Clark and Annie came down with just before Christmas this year, the double ear infection that stole nearly four entire nights of sleep from Clark as a one-year-old, the hand foot and mouth virus that sidelined our two for days last summer, or the sneaky devil we know as scarlet fever. Buckle up for a long story.

Although I always had a desire in my heart to be a full-time stay at home mom and was led to my current role because of many factors, managing sick children was a huge one. As a perfectionist, I have to feel as though I am doing the best job I am able to do at all times. If I can't, I struggle. When I went back to work part-time after having Annie, I struggled from the get go because I felt like I couldn't fully invest myself in a position when I was only there on given days. Add to this the reality that my crud buckets were always inevitably sick on the few days I was working…and it just didn't suit me.

While taking the plunge and committing to be at home full-time was a relief and something I wanted desperately, it created guilt in me as I was no longer making the hefty financial contribution to our household that I was accustomed to. Because of this, I started looking for occasional odd jobs that might somehow fit into our schedule only a few months after stepping away from nursing. During this search, however, I was summoned to jury duty for the first time in my life, and was quickly reminded that home is precisely where I am most needed and valued right now.

For starters, I tried to get out of said jury duty by contacting the local courthouse and making it known that I was the sole daytime care provider for both of my children and my niece. My request was big-time denied, but I was given permission to delay my week of service so that I would have time to make other arrangements. I took advantage of the delay, enlisted the daycare services of my in-laws and sisters, and proceeded to the courthouse a few months later. I'll be honest and say that I was a tiny bit excited for this opportunity for two reasons. The least selfish reason is that I truly wanted to see the workings of the judicial system in action and hoped to be called for a quick case. The remaining and super-selfish reason is that I was being forced into what I thought would be two or three quiet, reading-filled days away from my anything but quiet and reading-filled norm.

As the story of my life goes, however, guess who spent about a whopping five minutes perusing a magazine before being called into jury selection? Mmmm hmmm. This girl. Oh, and then guess who was selected to serve on the jury for the entire week…in a high-profile case no less that would keep jury members beyond typical courthouse hours without access to phones and an inability to communicate delays to the family members watching their children? That would be me again. The story doesn't end there, though. While I was already finding difficulty in not being able to connect with the outside world during court hours, Clark awoke midway through the week with a rash on his neck, chest and shoulders.

Because I was the second alternate amongst the jurors and knew that my opinions on the case would likely go unheard anyway, I again tried to talk my way out of service. I called the courthouse once more, explained the situation, and was politely informed that I would be able to call my son and check on him at lunchtime. I hastily phoned Jonathan, and while we determined that Clark was most likely having an allergic reaction to a new sunblock that he had used for the first time the day before, we decided it was probably best for Jonathan to take the rest of the day off and make a doctor's appointment to be safe. Jonathan started his 45-minute trek home, I temporarily left my spotted son in the capable hands of my father-in-law, and off I went to perform my civic duty.

Although Clark's pediatrician agreed that the rash was most likely an allergic reaction, he decided to culture him for strep. Clark had never had a fever nor complained of a sore throat to any degree, but the doctor just couldn't overlook the appearance of the rash. It looked like scarlet fever, and as it turns out, it very much was. Of course my poor child would silently battle strep throat and progress to scarlet fever the only five days of the year that my separation from him was mandatory and that I was essentially unreachable for updates[4]. Random crummies, as it turns out, are not very considerate. Random crummies suck.

Peanut butter and jelly. Yin and yang. Hugs and kisses. Germs and toddlers. They just go together. The toddler years are years strung together with spotty rashes, blistered mouths, goopy eyes, and yucky ears. Despite this, there is SO much good in the midst of the crud. So. Much. Good. All of these frequent childhood illnesses are simply the immune systems of toddlers learning how and what to battle. They're building up their defenses. They're learning to distinguish between friend and foe. And although it definitely feels endless in the moment when you're buying stock in Kleenex and Pedialyte...sickness itself actually *isn't* never-ending.

At nearly-three and four, I'm already starting to see signs of this with my kiddos. Of all of the toddler winters we've experienced thus far, this past year was the least germy by miles[5]. We said hello to the humidifier once or twice, of course, but we're a few weeks into spring at this point already and are mostly unscathed and intact. These days, illness has become much more sporadic and even when it does show its face, it is much less stressful. Because illness was a repeat offender for so much of the toddler stage, it turned Jonathan and me into sickness fighting pros who are unfazed by vomit and snot. Any color. Any amount. Any place. Bring it! If you're a cat herder and are treading water in a cesspool of toddler microbes, I promise that you'll come out a victor, too.

Far beyond the recognition that sickness is finite, however, is the realization that the accompanying snuggles are too. Germs may be the worst, but sick-kid snuggles—especially when your toddlers are movers like mine—are the absolute best. I love that when my kids are feeling their lowest, they want nothing more than the comfort and protection that mine and Jonathan's arms can offer. The mere fact that I get to play even a tiny role in helping them find relief is such a gift. It's beyond words, really. My toddlers are growing at rapid speed, and every day is one day closer to the day they don't want or need what my affection can provide. Because of this, I'll take the yuck. For as long as my babes want to cozy up with me on the couch and turn my sleeves into an abstract piece of art using snot as a medium…I'm down.

Footnotes

[1] When my babies were infants, there was one piece of equipment that I hated more than any other: the breast pump. That sucker was my nemesis, and I was more than ready to see it gone. The toddler years may be pump free around here, but OH do I have a new, possibly even greater archenemy. The *#$!*@?*&* humidifier. I can't stand the thing. Jonathan and I have owned a few varieties of this blasted tool and every time we end up with moldy, mildewy pieces no matter how often we change the water or how thoroughly we dry each part after washing. Or…we end up with melted plastic in the dishwasher when Whitney chooses not to heed warnings that items are not dishwasher safe. Oops. Anyway, Jonathan and I very literally just purchased a new humidifier today since our girl Annie, yet again, is barking overnight. This time we went bigger, watched videos online demonstrating the "ease" of cleaning, and have our fingers crossed that a better experience awaits. Wish us luck!

[2] If you've ever found yourself in the unfortunate place of dealing with a belly-sick toddler in the car, you know that it's super-duper gross and terribly smelly. Funny story for you: Jonathan's family has an annual brunch the morning after Thanksgiving. Last year, my brother and sister-in-law weren't able to make it and asked if Jonathan and I would be able to take Madison along. We were happy to do so, and helped to ensure that Madison enjoy a variety of goodies from the buffet…all of which made a second appearance on the floor of our car only an hour or so later. While it wasn't a fun experience for our poor sweetie or for my champ of a hubby who put in the elbow grease to clean up the mess after we got home, let me just say that orange juice, apparently, has the ability to make vomit smell rather lovely. As poor Madison retched away into the zip-top bag I hastily dumped pretzels from in order to fashion a barf bag out of after her first eruption, I got a big whiff of the citrusy smell greeting my nostrils and said to Jonathan: "Well, I suppose it could be worse! Her barf smells pretty good, actually." Thank God for OJ.

[3] A few months back, Annie spiked a fever in the 104 range overnight. Because her temperature was so high and we wanted to make sure that the medication we had just given would be effective, Jonathan and I decided to put Annie between us in our bed. Conversations with Annie are always comical, but 3 AM conversations impacted by fever and exhaustion—conversations about nipples, of course—are especially funny.

[4] Oh, and in case you're wondering, I remained the second alternate throughout the duration of that case, sat sequestered for hours of jury deliberation, and was formally dismissed three days later than the remainder of the pool I started the week with.

[5] Obviously, now that I've typed those words and made it official, Clark and Annie will at some point cover me in vomit today, but for now it's true at least.

6 THE BLACK HOLE THAT IS WINTER

People who visit Pennsylvania say that it's verdant and beautiful. People who visit Pennsylvania say that it must be so lovely to live in a state that experiences all four seasons. People who *do* live in Pennsylvania, though? Well, people who live in Pennsylvania see things differently. Yes, we see the green and we love ourselves some spring blossoms, summer suns, fall leaves, and winter snows, but these things are only half of the story. In Pennsylvania, we don't experience four seasons. We experience eight. We have the nice part of spring when everyone temporarily welcomes new life… and then we have the allergy-filled part of spring when everyone curses it. We have the nice part of summer when everyone temporarily welcomes the heat…and then we have the humid part of summer when everyone loathes it. We have the nice part of fall when everyone temporarily welcomes the cool…and then we have the damp part of fall when everyone is disgusted by it. And last but certainly not least, we have the nice part of winter when everyone temporarily welcomes the snow…and then we have the FRIGGIN-COLD part of winter when everyone is made miserable by it.

I am not a winter person. I am not a let's dress in layers person. I am not a let's find something to do inside because our ears will fall off if we go outside person. While I super-love Christmas with all of its hype and its festive accompaniments and do look forward to an occasional snow day and the fun it brings for my children, I much prefer the days of the year that allow me to walk to my mailbox wearing the same thing I slept in and soak up far too much UV radiation while my toddlers expend their energy under the sky. Like Clark and Annie, I thrive when I can breathe in fresh air and absorb vitamin D from the sun. Winter months in Pennsylvania simply deprive us of the things we love best…far, far too often[1].

If you are a person who lives somewhere that's warm all year long, I applaud you. I am also majorly envious of you and maybe hate you just the teensiest ounce of a bit (joking!), but you are living life right. The toddler struggles I am about to jump into pertain to all things winter. Colder-than-cold wind chills. Snow that is messier than it is fun. Layers of clothing that never end. Cabin Fever to the max. These sorts of things. If winter has never been an experience you've endured with toddlers in the mix, you may not relate to all of what follows…but I promise you can laugh at it anyway.

Before I had children, winter was just something that I had a casual distaste for. We were sort of on neutral terms. Since I became a parent, though? Our relationship isn't quite so lackluster. Today, I think it's safe to say that winter and I have a heated repulsion for one another. I dread its arrival, and I am always happy to say adios to it come March (or April or May as Mother Nature is a tease around here). Replacing sunblock for gloves and ear warmers makes my heart cry a little, and let it be known that a recovery of my internet search history over the winter months always includes looking for jobs and real estate in locations that are far warmer and more coastal in nature.

Now that my toddlers are a part of the picture, getting outside isn't just something that I enjoy or look forward to, it's something we all *need* to preserve our sanity. While winter used to have me missing and longing for surroundings other than my home or my place of employment, winters today bring me to phoning every hotel in the near vicinity with an indoor pool. Why, you ask? Oh, because I beg them all to allow me and my children to come swimming. Just in case you're thinking this sounds like a good idea and would like to try it yourself come next December, please know that my requests are always shot down. I have, however, come pretty darn close to purchasing a night's stay on more than one occasion. Whether that stay would be for family access to the pool or for me to hide myself in solace for 24 hours is for me to know and you (not) to find out. Ha.

In the Bausman household, all parties are happier people if and when the sun is shining. Annie, like her Daddy, needs time outside because she loves and appreciates everything that nature offers her. This girl has an affinity for all things living more so than I have ever witnessed. She adores plants, insects, and animals alike. Hand her a rattlesnake, and she'd make a best friend out of it. Last summer, I kid you not that a wasp or bee or some sort of stinging creature landed right beside Annie on the deck of my mom's pool and instead of crying or fleeing or panicking as would any of her female cousins, she got down on all fours, put her nose within an inch of the sucker and happily declared the following:

"Heh-wo dare wittle bug!"

If you need translation, that's *"Hello there little bug!"* in Annie-talk. Fearing that Annie was about to smooch her new-found bestie as is often the case, I shouted this response:

"Annie Nadean, do NOT touch or kiss that bug. That bug bites!"

Annie loves animals. She gets animals. She speaks animal. We often dog-sit for a cuter-than-cute, nicer-than-nice pup named Dexter, and if Jonathan or I can't get a homesick Dex to eat his dinner…we hand it over to Annie. She locks eyes with Dexter, says whatever it is she says to him without making a single sound, sits the bowl in front of him, and he happily inhales it all. Just recently, Annie asked me if she could have baby ladybugs come to her upcoming birthday party, and I may even be considering hatching her some baby chicks. If this girl doesn't grow up to be a veterinarian or a zoologist, I'll be amazed. She's something special.

Like his sister, Clark also needs and benefits from sunshine, but not because he is a lover of critters. For Clark, his outdoor passion is his bicycle. Remember my frugal ways? Well a few years back, basically before he even walked with stability, I purchased a little balance bike for five dollars at a yard sale for my guy. Laugh away, but it had been run over by a car…hence the price. The front wheel remains a little wonky even to this day, but I assure you that we've gotten our money's worth times about a million on this thing. If you aren't familiar with balance bikes, they're like toddler sized versions of traditional, two-wheeled bikes but they lack pedals. Basically, the tot on board uses his or her legs to give momentum and to brake. Last summer, Clark took off on it and hasn't stopped since. He's got his balance bike fully accessorized now with blinking headlights and taillights, and recently found and attached a jingle-bell Christmas tree ornament for good measure. Just about every pair of shoes Clark owns are worn at the toe from taking one too many spins on his beloved bike. Living on a quarter-mile circle has become quite beneficial to us as of late.

When winter's wrath robs us of conversations with bugs and bicycle rides, we all get a little bit crabby under our roof. Stir-craziness sets in, hostilities rise, and tempers shorten. As you recall, this is also the prime time of year for illnesses to pop up, which results in heightened stress and lack of proper, restful sleep. As you *also* recall, sleepiness begets crankiness. It's a vicious cycle. Outside days that are filled with warmth and sunshine seem to go so quickly. Too quickly. They are days filled with sidewalk chalk, swing sets, and bubbles, and in the blink of an eye the sun is setting. Inside, cold-weather days, however? Well, the cooped-up days feel long and draggy somehow even though the sun sets at like a depressing 4 PM. These days leave toddler parents longing for bedtime. I love my children beyond words, but draggy winter days are rough. I play a mean game of Memory and can Pop See Ko with mad skills, but I can only take so much 'kid stuff' before I reach my breaking point.

Winter's unkind and drawn-out ways have led me, unfortunately, to many a mommy meltdown. Several chapters back, we talked at great length about toddlers and their tantrums. We've already established that my toddlers can hold their own when it comes to tantrums, but I'll be the first to admit that I can too. I'd be a liar if I said that my meltdowns were reserved only for the winter months, but pasty-pale, vitamin D deficient, cold-to-the-core Whitney is at a far greater likelihood of breaking down than is a beach-bronzed, vitamin-stocked, warm Whitney. Do you remember how I said that I can't be held accountable for the things I say and do when I am hungry and tired? Well, I'd like to add to this list. Anything I say or do during the winter months must be exempt from judgment too. I'd like to propose that if someone can plead insanity to a crime, I can plead winter. Just saying.

One saving grace about winter is that I truly LOVE the holiday season. Christmas is my jam, and I adore the lights, the music, the cookies, and the spirit of giving. Salvation Army bell ringing? Let me at it. Watching Elf on repeat? You know it. Busting out the NSYNC Christmas album a week before Thanksgiving? Oh, yeah. Christmas makes me giddy, turns me into the biggest kid every December, and overhauls my dreams with visions of tinsel and candy canes. Even holidays are troublesome with toddlers in the picture, however. Why? Well, because holidays bring with them parties and family gatherings that take place in other peoples' homes. Homes where Clark and Annie love to run rampant and cause me all sorts of stress. Attending parties and get-togethers with toddlers in tow can be challenging. It can cause moms and dads to ask themselves the following questions:

-What will they break here?

-How could they kill themselves here?

OR

-Why did we even come here?

Sometimes, attending parties with toddlers is a whole lot more damage control, peer mediation, and surveillance than it is time with other adults, conversation, or socialization. If I'm being honest, there has definitely been such an event or two that left Jonathan and me feeling more drained and exhausted than in any sort of holiday spirit.

Apart from the holiday season, there is one more thing about winter that I actually enjoy, but it comes with a stipulation. You know how sometimes kitty companions adore belly rubs but only for a precise five seconds before they start digging their claws into your skin? Like my toddlers, apparently I possess a feline trait or two because I love a good, sizable snow every year...but only exactly once. Pennsylvania snows tend to not abide by my stipulation. Pennsylvania snows are just stupid.

In Pennsylvania, we get a lot of un-fun, un-pretty snows that end up being more of an icy, slushy driving nuisance than anything worth looking at or playing in. In Pennsylvania, we sort of live in this in-between zone where the threat of monster storms always looms— sending folks into a milk, egg, and bread purchasing panic at every grocery store across the state on a weekly basis from December through March—yet we rarely get hammered with white. Pennsylvania winters leave me in a constant state of anticipation and subsequent let down.

When we do get a few inches of snow—even if it's a sloppy, messy snow or even if little, stinging ice balls are actively being pelted from the sky—I'm the first one to gear my kids up and GET THEM OUT. We find fun in using food coloring to 'paint' the snow, in making snowballs with which to sling at one another[2], in constructing snowmen that look all sorts of interesting, and in ignoring child labor laws in order to put our toddlers to work at shoveling. Gearing them up to get out, though? Not super fun.

While I will concede that my children are usually a little less resistant to the concept of getting dressed when they know the end result is going outside to play in the snow, they still remain the furthest thing from being willing and cooperative participants. Typically, my efforts zero in on Madison first since she's the easiest and least likely to resist. After I get her bundled up, then I start my bargaining with Clark and ensure that I've selected the right color of gloves, the most comfortable pair of snow pants, and the proper boots. After Clark is squared away, I hunt down Annie and then wrap myself around her while I add layers enough to turn her into a blob. After I properly dress myself and we are a solid 20 to 25 minutes into the process, we are finally at a point of conclusion[3]. Until we realize that going potty *first* was forgotten, that is. Back to square one.

Even without snow, winter clothing layers are annoying and cumbersome. In the summertime, my toddlers can roll outside wearing next to nothing. We're talking bare feet, a simple pair of cotton shorts, and a t-shirt. Heck, I'm even good with just underwear. This, in turn, means that I have a lot less herding, wrangling, restraining, and dressing to manage. In the winter, though? In the winter, the preservation of my children's ears, nose, fingers, and toes depends on how I dress them. Talk about pressure. Oh, and don't forget about our toddler straight jacket, the car seat. Car seat struggles are already very real without bulky clothing in the mix. For matters of both ease and of safety, the car seat is an even bigger battle to fight in cold-weather months.

So, how do we combat all of these winter struggles? How do we combat Cabin Fever, cold temperatures, and layer upon layer of clothing? Well, we get creative. My sisters think I am five parts crazy and make fun of me often, but I do just about anything and everything it takes to continue getting my children outside all year long. If there aren't weather alerts suggesting that my toddlers may be subjected to frostbite should we brave the elements, out we go. We don piles of clothing to degrees that somewhat hinder mobility, and we head to the park anyway. We may fall down a ladder here or there when our 14 pairs of pants impact how easily our little legs bend, but no worries. Clothing layers also serve as cushions.

Long winters and long winter days have certainly gotten the best of me from time to time during the toddler years. In full disclosure, there have even been winter days that have been overwhelming to the point that I wanted to cry uncle and lock my bedroom door for an hour or two (or twelve). When you aren't a winter person from the get-go, winter only gets more challenging with toddlers in the picture. It just does. The sunshine you long for and the warmth you miss deeply are missed all the more when you're confined inside the walls of your home with little beings who haven't breathed fresh air or properly burnt off their piles of energy in days.

What I say to all of this, however, is that although already-long winters may feel even longer with toddlers present, winters with toddlers truly are better. For starters, when the shorter days and cold temperatures have me feeling a little blue, *nothing* on Earth can warm my heart more than a perfectly-timed *"I love you momma!"* or an unprompted hug from either Clark or Annie. I find more value in those things than the sun itself. Oh, and as far as the stressful holiday parties go? Well, I promise that eventually you'll be able to ship those toddlers down to the basement to play without fearing that the entire house will implode. Believe it or not, Jonathan and I have been a part of many a family gathering lately where we've actually been able to talk with other adults, eat our meals without inhaling them at lightning speed, and drive away at the end of the night feeling refreshed and proud of Clark and Annie for how nicely they behaved and played. Winning! Parties aside, the holiday season is just so much more special in and of itself as a parent. For me, this is one of the very best parts of having little people to care for.

The year before we had Clark, I'll never forget waking with Jonathan on Christmas morning and almost feeling lonely or bored. I loved Christmases with my husband and truly enjoyed the holidays we were able to celebrate as 'just' a couple, but together, we simply felt like something was missing. Something *was* missing. We were missing our crazy, busy, beautiful, yet-to-be Clark and Annie. Little did we know that Clark was already growing inside of me on that Christmas morning, and little did we know that Christmas would never again be lacking. My toddlers may make Christmas a little extra exhausting, but oh do they make it magical. Christmas now brings with it new traditions, new discoveries, and new perspectives. I love that Jonathan and I are able to both teach and demonstrate to our children that Christmas is far more than a day or a guy wearing a red suit. It's a reminder to put others first, to cherish people more than things, and to find warmth in the comfort of family…even when it's miserably cold and sunless outside.

I love my family deeply, and I love that I have the three of them to keep me warm when the weather is anything but. Even though they seem endless, winters come to a close, days grow longer, flowers bloom, and sunshine prevails. When winter rolls around next year, I know it'll hit me again as it always does and that a few mopey days lie in wait, but I also know that I've got everything I need to keep me cozy until spring.

Post-Script

Very intentionally, I made sure that this was the shortest chapter of *Herding Cats*. The thieving winter months rob me of the warmth I crave, so I refuse to give them an overabundance of real estate here. Take that, Mother Nature!

Footnotes

[1] This is the point at which the readers out there in places that get much colder than Pennsylvania even on its coldest day are rolling their eyes and calling me out. Yes, I know, I am a baby with little to actually complain about. I accept it! FYI, you guys are just nuts. Do you know that places exist where you can walk from your car to the inside of the grocery store without the risk of losing a digit in January? Kidding! You all know I have nothing but love (and concern) for you.

[2] Earlier this year, I awoke one morning to find a honking, nasty-looking, deeper-than-deep purple bruise on my left hip. For the life of me, I couldn't recall any sort of provoking injury. Jonathan caught a glimpse of my newly-acquired body paint and concernedly asked what had happened. Upon visualizing his face, my mind was flooded with memories. Memories of a snowball fight from the previous evening. Memories of when my mean husband created a very densely packed ~~snow~~ ice ball with which to wallop me. Do you see the abuse I endure? HA! No, in all honesty it was a bunch of good fun, and I look forward to retaliation in the future. You've been warned, lover.

[3] At this point, our crew clumsily heads toward the garage where someone always inevitably trips and falls down the step regardless of our level of caution. It's difficult to function when you look like a colorful marshmallow.

7 THINGS RELATING TO SLEEP

When Jonathan and I made the decision to forego our days of childlessness, we knew full well that sleeping as we knew it was a thing of the past. We knew that newborns entered the world with hungry bellies which needed filling 24 hours a day, and we knew that 'sleeping in' would be a lost luxury. We wanted it anyway. We wanted the long nights, the wake-up calls, and the exhaustion because we wanted what came with it. Things like snuggles and tiny toes and new baby smells. We knew that the cute and the good and the beautiful things were packaged with other things that were less attractive and a whole lot more fatiguing, but we wanted and got it all.

While it's true that the newborn stage was harder in terms of sleeping simply because there was so little of it to be had for us, we expected those struggles. I don't think either of us, however, suspected the sleep-related shenanigans we currently tackle on a daily basis with our toddlers. Our struggles are very far from over. Clark and Annie, as it turns out, are sleep-avoiding, sleep-delaying, sleep-defying masters. Clearly, they did NOT inherit this trait from their mother...

I think what it all boils down to for my children when it comes to sleep is what we've already touched on a few times: they are always in motion. Whether it be their bodies, their mouths, or their minds, the wheels of Clark and Annie are just always turning. Sleep inherently goes against their nature. I almost feel like settling down into slumber signifies defeat to them some days. Because of this, they fight the notion of 'giving in'. Even when they're tired-tired, Clark and Annie go. I would say, in fact, that they go even faster and harder under the strain of fatigue. While it would seem most logical for a toddler to slow with exhaustion, this is the very opposite of truth for both Clark and his sister. They get fidgety. They get loud. They get reckless[1].

Annie, especially, is always-always moving regardless of her level of alertness. My mom jokes that Annie doesn't know how to walk, in fact, because…Annie doesn't walk. Annie runs. I can't even tell you the amount of times in a week this child's poor knees are scuffed or scraped or bruised. The combination of her master-level speed and her amateur-level coordination renders her quite accident prone…especially when she is combating sleepiness. A tired Annie is a clumsy Annie. Despite this, very little keeps her down. She frequently wipes out, comes up bloodied and battle-scarred and simply says, "*I'm OK!*"

Because of how much energy they expend, how rapidly they grow, and how much brain power they exhaust on a daily basis, sleep is an essential and vital component of a toddler's day and night. The toddler years, however, are problematic years in terms of sleeping. Why? Well, for a variety of reasons. First and foremost, these years are tough and transitional because of the loss of a dearly-loved piece of furniture. The crib.

Yes, my relationship with the crib was love-hate at times[2], but let me just tell you that I miss that son of a gun pretty profoundly some days. I know that there are a lot of folks out there who have a purely hate-hate relationship with cribs and all that they stand for, are proponents of co-sleeping, and who deem cribs an unkind prison. I get it, I in no way judge, and I say do what works for you…but I am not one of those people. While confinement is other people's beef with cribs, confinement was my salvation.

Clark has been an early riser for as long as I can remember. He is up with the sun and ready to rock long before I would ideally choose for him to wake. Clark still rose super early when he slept in a crib, but it was the safe confinement of it that allowed Daddy and me to delay our own awakening. On weekends or other occasions when Jonathan and I didn't have to start our days as early because of work and getting Clark over to Ashley's, we would check the battery life on his favorite little crib toy before putting him down for bed, add in a book or two, and let him play in his crib while we slumbered on the next morning. For as busy of a baby as Clark was and as busy of a toddler as Clark still is, he loved the comfort and protection and isolation of his crib and thrived with that balance of independent time. Clark never tried to climb out of his crib, and Jonathan and I actually cut that cord when we deemed him ready. Annie, however…well, Annie was an entirely different story.

Clark and Annie balance one another out when it comes to sleep-related happenings, it seems. Clark slept through the night at a very young age…somewhere around eight weeks old. Annie, though, continued to wake at least once every night until she was closer to eight *months* old. Clark is always up early. Annie sleeps in. Clark would have stayed in his crib indefinitely. Annie was out of hers, in a very literal sense, before she was even two years old.

Unlike Clark, Annie is my sleeper-inner. When she was confined to her crib, she would go to bed without much of a protest by 8 PM and sleep well beyond 9 AM the following morning. Dreamy, right?? Even when she woke, Annie would entertain herself, babble away, and play in her crib happily until I'd remember that she still existed. I won't lie…there was definitely a time or two where Clark and I were well into our days and distracted with some sort of activity when I looked at the clock, noticed that it was nearly 11 AM, and hadn't yet set Annie free of her captivity. Oops. Plain and simple: crib life was awesome while it lasted.

Sadly for me, however, Annie is quite a fearless little girl with a knack for escaping restraint. Car seats. Clothing. We've already covered those. Well, she escaped the crib too. Very, very early. Around the age of 18 months old, I once found Annie napping on her floor outside of her crib. The floor, mind you, was most definitely not where I laid her down. Since she wasn't hurt and I was clearly in denial, I did what all good parents do. I pretended it didn't happen. Fortunately, this was a fluke occurrence that went without repeating itself for another couple of months…but those months were just not long enough for me. At 22 months of age, Annie decided to make it known that she was not staying put any longer.

Jonathan and Clark were at my father-in-law's cottage for an annual getaway they call 'Fishing Weekend', and Annie and I were at home enjoying our time together without the boys. After a long morning of running errands and playing, I put Annie down for a nap only to hear the pitter pat of little feet on the floor a few moments later. Again, I was Super Mom, ignored her daring feat/feet, scooped her up, plopped her back in her crib, and watched with bated breath on the monitor to see what would unfold. Within moments, up went her little, chubby leg, over went her hips, and she was out. Again. The crib days were over.

Transitioning Clark to a 'big boy bed' was so much easier and less stressful than was that same transition with Annie because he was older and truly ready. Annie was anything but ready to have so much freedom, but we didn't have a choice. Safety concerns trump Mommy's and Daddy's preferences, sadly. We started Annie with a mattress on the floor, but for months our girl slept in front of her door right on the carpet. It was half pathetic and half hilarious, but it worked about as good as it could and eventually our climber made her way onto her 'bed'.

The consistent, safe stability of the crib and what it offered both me and my babes was what I loved best about it. While my kids really did adapt and adjust better than I expected both times around when this furniture friend was gone, there was still a loss of a certain level of security and a whole new set of "what if's" to overcome. Beyond the crib, however, there is another stable friend that tends to come and go during toddlerhood in the world of sleep. Would anyone like to make a guess? I'll give you some hints. It's one of the few things that even feisty felines are fond of, and it rhymes with 'crap slime'. Guys, seriously, I shouldn't be allowed to write books. Ha. Anyway, yes, I'm talking about nap time.

In the parenting world—and extra especially in the stay-at-home parenting world—nap time is akin to the Holy Grail. It is sacred, it is sought after, and it is more precious than diamonds. During the newborn months, solid, *predictable* chunks of nap time are something that are acquired over time with patience, persistence, and lots of discovering what does and doesn't work. Consistent infant naps are an achievement. When I had newborns, control-freak me put in effort the first 12 months of my children's lives to establish routines and schedules as much as possible. It will surprise you 0% to hear that I am not one to fly by the seat of my pants. I have friends who are absolutely stress-free, low-maintenance, let's-see-what-happens-today parents who have equally adaptive, flexible, and carefree kiddos. While I admire, respect and give mad kudos to them, my personality just doesn't lend itself to chance[3]. I wanted and needed as much structure as I could feasibly grasp. It took repeated cycles of trial and error to get to a point of consistency by any means, but by the time Clark and Annie transitioned from infants to toddlers, they were fairly reliable in their daytime sleeping and slid into one long, afternoon nap seamlessly. Generally speaking and with time, Clark and Annie excelled at toddler napping.

Because of how hard they go during their waking hours, taking a nap is of huge benefit to my toddlers. They aren't the only beneficiaries of afternoon rest, however. Like many parents of the world, *I* benefit from nap time, too. Nap time is my chance to regroup, determine whether or not an attitude adjustment is needed as I head into the afternoon and evening hours, get caught up on housework and cooking responsibilities, and, if I'm in the middle of writing as I am now, put my fingers to the keyboard. At alarming speeds, though, time is passing. Every time I glance Clark's way, I swear he's grown an inch. Each and every day now, he looks much less like the toddler he was a few months ago and much more like the young boy he is quickly becoming.

At the age of four, Clark is currently outgrowing nap time. Needless to say, it's been a season of transition around here, and transitions—as we know—are not always fun. Hanging until bedtime without a nap has been a challenge for everyone involved. Basically by dinner time, Clark has about zero attention span, no focus, and an inability to sit still. Sadly for him and frustratingly for me, dinner just so happens to require attention, focus, and stillness. While the process could be simple and two-step: 1. Sit, 2. Eat...it has been anything but as of late. Clark falls out of his chair an inexplicable amount of times. He needs to use the bathroom at least once. He recalls that he left the light on in the basement and insists that it be turned off immediately. He has to run over to the window to see which neighbor just drove by...and so on and so on. Daddy and I have been a little extra stressed lately. Be nice to us, World.

Speaking of this, you know when the world isn't nice to us? Three words for you: Daylight Savings Time. I understand the need for well-lit working hours and you and I both know how much I love me some sunshine, but why do we need to change the clocks twice a year in order to achieve this? Much like winter, Daylight Savings Time wasn't as big of a deal for me before I had kids. I won't say that I particularly loved the thought of losing an hour of sleep every spring or working an extra hour as a night-shift nurse every fall, but all in all I adapted and overcame. I didn't care *that* much. With toddlers on board, though, I care that much and more. Daylight Savings Time is yet another toddler sleeping struggle.

A few years ago when our country was nearing a certain presidential election, I posted the following on Facebook:

Just keeping it real (and lighthearted). While many of you are fretting over the upcoming election, I have relented any sense of control on that matter and am, instead, fretting over the upcoming event called Daylight Savings Time. This is the 'super cool' time of year when my son who already wakes at 5 AM may start waking at 4 AM. Maybe I need to start drinking caffeine again. ASAP.

This pretty much sums up my thoughts on Daylight Savings Time, and guess what? I did start drinking caffeine again only a short while later. I can't say for sure that it was the clock change that led me to this decision, but I'm going to say it had something to do with it.

One thing I know for sure that was impacted by Daylight Savings Time was a life-changing purchase. Because Clark already rose like a rooster and was only more inclined to do so after winding the clocks back an hour in the fall, I was desperate for something that would help my guy understand the difference between what an appropriate waking hour was and the nonsense he was trying to pull. In those days, I was still getting up once overnight between 3 and 4 AM to feed Annie only to fall back asleep just long enough to be in a state of delirium when Clark would show up at my bedside no more than an hour later. Because of this, I hopped on the net and started searching for solutions.

What I eventually came to purchase was what is called an 'OK to Wake' clock. On the whole, toddlers cannot tell time and simply don't have the capacity to look at a clock and determine whether or not it is alright for them to rise and shine. 'OK to Wake' clocks, however, use something toddlers can understand because they are able to visualize it clearly: light change. At the time of my choosing, Clark's clock lights up green and signifies to him that he has permission to leave his room and come find Jonathan or me. I'm telling you. It's worth its weight in gold.

From the very first day we possessed Clark's 'OK to Wake' clock, we had closed bedroom doors until 7 AM. I know 7 AM is still ungodly early for some of you parents out there with sleeper-inners, but 7 AM was and is pure bliss for me. When Annie was still waking overnight and I was desperate for a bit more shut eye, a 7 AM kick-off to the day meant almost two entire hours' worth of extra sleep. Today, now that sleeping through the night is something we almost always achieve without issue[4], a 7 AM kick-off to the day means that I can get up when Jonathan does for work and have silent, glorious, coffee-filled moments to get myself in gear before my eyes are graced with the sights of my chatty cherubs. It goes without saying that the 'OK to Wake' clock has practically achieved idol status in our home as it makes wake-up and getting out of bed a whole lot simpler. Now if only there could be a contraption that made getting children *in* bed easier...

Just a few paragraphs back, I made the statement that Clark and Annie excelled at toddler napping, which is/was true. I have to clarify things for you, however, before I progress in this discussion. While Clark and Annie have, for the most part, been solid sleepers when sleep is actually achieved, it's the *getting there* part that always requires effort. Like a ton of effort. I'm talking sweat-inducing effort. When my best friend Kelly gave birth to her firstborn Colton seven months ago, one of the first things I told her to savor was the bedtime process with Colt before he becomes mobile and vocal. Before our babes could talk back and run away from us, nap time and bedtime were tender. They involved sweet little songs and stories, a rocking chair, snuggles, and soothing voices. Today, however, the nap time and bedtime process is chaotic at best. It involves songs that are interrupted, repeated threats that little bottoms must actually sit still to listen to stories, and voices that progressively get louder and more threatening as breaking points are met and exceeded.

Bedtime especially is a beast under our roof. Bedtime is simply unachievable until we've read two stories, prayed, sang four songs in a precise order...at a precise volume...and at a precise speed, have discussed the following day's happenings, and have shouted "*good night!*" from the hallway a good 10 times. No exaggeration. On top of this, both Clark and Annie have become Olympic-level stalling champions. My toddlers will toss out any and every excuse they can imagine in order to put a halt on any progress towards slumber. These excuses are all over the map from needing a spoonful of honey to ward off overnight coughs—even when there are no coughs to be had—to needing to peek out the front window to ensure that our solar-powered hummingbird is functional and illuminated. Overall, however, drinks and potty visits are the most frequented culprits here. Bedtime in the Bausman home, apparently, is a thirst-inducing and bladder-awakening experience.

If you're Annie, though, there are many more ways to stall bedtime apart from requesting a trip to the bathroom. If you're Annie, you have about 42 more ways. Your bedmates. Clark and Annie's beds contrast starkly, and it's just downright funny. Clark's bed is barren. These days, he's got one pillow and one comforter. Case closed[5]. Annie's bed, though? Oh my goodness. Annie's bed is anxiety-inducing to my less-is-more, neat freak soul. Annie's bed is home to six security blankets, no less than a dozen stuffed animals, and a revolving assortment of random odds and ends including books, doll accessories, and even a pretzel or two from time to time. True to her nature, Annie essentially sleeps with a menagerie of animal friends, and believe me when I say that she knows if and when any one of them is missing. Every night, Jonathan and I get to play a game of hide and go seek with one or more of Annie's plush pals or perform a scavenger hunt around the house to find a blankie gone rogue. It's maddening.

Why does all of this stuff matter anyway? Why does it matter how long it takes to herd our cats into their beds if they do ultimately sleep the whole night through? Well, because for as selfish as it sounds, Jonathan and I NEEEEEEEEEED the down time that becomes ours when Clark and Annie dream about gummy bears or whatever it is that toddlers dream about. I hope you don't mishear me on this one because while, yes, it is very much true that I have been known to skip through the halls of my home with my arms outstretched singing songs of celebration when sleep on the part of my toddlers is finally achieved for the night[6], I am also all-in when they're awake. In my opinion anyway, if I ensure that my children are well cared for, know beyond a doubt that they are loved and cherished, and are given as much quality time and attention with me as is possible during their waking hours (given that our house still needs to be standing at the end of the day), I sort of earn the right to covet the freedom that their slumber offers me.

For Jonathan and me, the hours after Clark and Annie are settled for the night and before our own heads hit the pillow are 'our time' as a couple. Yes, of course, we communicate throughout the day via text while he's at work and speak to one another in the presence of the kids when he gets home, but this is when we have a chance for real, uninterrupted conversation. Additionally, this is when we have a chance to binge-watch our favorite shows on Netflix and eat our obligatory and much-adored evening popcorn. There's an interesting dynamic to these hours because in all reality, Jonathan and I are exhausted enough to go to bed ourselves the very minute Clark and Annie's bedroom doors close. Despite this, we typically choose time together and set off for the couch to unwind.

When you have toddlers, unwinding becomes very necessary as parents. More often than not, this unwinding occurs when those active, talkative, always needing something toddlers are sleeping. While it is a simple concept in and of itself, sleep, unfortunately, is not always the simplest achievement. Sleep-related challenges and struggles are often a part of the picture when it comes to toddlers. It's a package deal. Sleep may not be as straightforward as it seems in a home that contains a toddler, but the takeaway here? The takeaway sure is.

Sooner than later, the night will come when Clark or Annie tells me for the first time that they don't need or want to be tucked in. Sooner than later, there will be no more bedtime stories, no more bedtime prayers, and no more bedtime snuggles. Sooner than later, all of the obstacles that Jonathan and I face now—the search for missing stuffies and the requests for *"just one more sip"* of water—are going to end. Sooner than later, it will be a simple, boring alarm clock that wakes me every morning in place of the beautiful and precious face of my child. Sooner than later, I truly believe that I will miss each and every part of the moments that seem so tough and frustrating right now. Sooner than later, guys.

For as much as I can't wait for my toddlers to be in bed some evenings, you want to hear the truth? Even on those evenings, I find myself missing them—truly missing their nonsense, their quirks, their hilarity, and just their presence—the second they're asleep. Every night without fail, Jonathan and I start our silent hours by recapping the memorable things that escaped our toddlers' lips that day, and with so much material, we always have a lot to laugh at. More than I love sleep or love the idea of my kids sleeping, I love what Clark and Annie bring to my life…including their unparalleled sense of humor. I love the energy they simultaneously consume and give off, and I love the purpose they have gifted me with. On the nights when bedtime looks a whole lot like a circus performance, may I resolve to remember that the circus won't always be in town. It's certainly in town today, tomorrow, next week, and probably even a good six months from now…but even circuses don't last forever.

Footnotes

[1] The Pannuccis, who you've already met, have a term for this that I love. They call it getting 'slappy'. Lillie Jane is much like my two in that she gets amped when she is tired. Slappiness has been a part of many a Pannucci play-date. With so many like-minded toddlers to choose from, at least one is bound to be tired at all times…

[2] Our predominant struggles with the crib were limbs wedged in between the slats and wee ones who figured out how to pull themselves up to standing long before they learned how to let go and lay back down.

[3] Neither does Jonathan's. Jonathan is a first born in every sense of the term and I, being born five years after my middle sister, am what is known as a 'gap child'. Instead of possessing the traits of a last born, which I am, I tend to possess more of the traits

commonly associated with first borns or only children. Perfectionism. Conscientiousness. Structure. Control. Sound familiar? How Jonathan and I make our relationship work when we share the same mind is beyond me, but we do. I love this guy.

[4] Never make statements like this publicly. Without fail, they bite you in the tush. Just about as soon as my fingers typed those words a few days back, Annie decided that a sleep regression was due. Bad dreams, thirst, and having to go potty are currently on my short list of enemies.

[5] A few months back, Clark banned all stuffed animals from his room without explanation and never invited them back. From that point onward, there was only his security blanket to keep him company. Just recently, however, Clark had to sever ties with his beloved 'bee-boo' as it was a stumbling block in his road to thumb-sucking sobriety. Clark has been a thumb sucker since he was about 6 months old, and although it was never a daytime problem, it certainly was a nighttime one. At the past two dental visits, there was noted shifting in Clark's teeth related to this habit, so Jonathan and I purchased and utilized overnight thumb guards to keep our guy's thumbs out of his mouth. Give him a high five the next time you see him! He's in recovery.

[6] In case you're wondering, my go-to song is one that I fabricated myself. You take the Christmas tune that says "It's the most wonderful time of the year…" and make it work for bedtime with toddlers. It goes like this… "It's the most wonderful time of the day!" Catchy, huh?

8 THE GLORY DAYS OF POTTY TRAINING

Once upon a time, a slew of grown adults and one tiny, potty-training toddler packed themselves into a car. They got situated, settled in, and set off for an annual fair approximately 45 minutes from home. The voyage itself was uneventful, and there was relative peace on the road. The same could not be said, however, for the proceedings that unfolded after the group arrived at their destination. What followed next was a far cry from peace. What followed next was uproar. Why? Because of the conflict between the toddler's bite-sized bladder and his smorgasbord-sized opinions.

Upon spending no more than five minutes at the fair, the toddler announced that a visit to the bathroom was needed. The toddler made that visit with his father soon thereafter, but he boldly proclaimed that the facilities available were just 'too scary'. The father tried to calm the child's fears in order to garner success, but the toddler—in true toddler style—would not relent. The defeated man and the full-bladdered child returned to the group and provided an update on the unfolding situation. When the toddler's mother chimed in and insisted that the bathroom be visited again, the child transformed into an irate creature. In an instant, everyone in the immediate vicinity became aware of the group's troubles. The father and mother tried bargaining and bribery without success. At this, they resorted to threats. The child's parents insisted that the entire group would be forced to leave the fair if the toddler chose not to use the bathroom. And the toddler? Naturally, he chose not to use the bathroom anyway. Because the parents were the sort to follow through, their threats were not empty. When the toddler and his brick wall defenses refused to return to the restroom, there was an abrupt ending to an evening that had barely even begun.

The group, hungry and disappointed, started the trek back to their car. Only steps away from where the car was parked, a lawn lay covered in odds and ends. It was a yard sale. Most of what was spread on that lawn was forgettable and without importance, but one thing—one salvation-providing thing—caught the father's eye. Lo and behold! There was a toddler potty for sale. And not just *any* toddler potty, mind you. The very same potty that the child was accustomed to using at home. The father hunted down the homeowner, asked if he could purchase the Godsend of a gift, and secured the most worthy and gratifying transaction of his life. Cash traded hands, and within mere seconds, the tiny toilet was put to use. After a few internal sighs of relief and Huzzah!'s, the group made its way back to the fair where an evening of food and fun awaited.

What are the odds, right? What are the odds that in a moment when stubbornness, defeat, and discomfort were colliding…the universe saw fit to plop a perfectly-placed plastic pot right where it was needed most. For as unlikely as it seems, I didn't embellish this story in the least. Right hand to the Bible, it all happened. Every bit of it. You may be asking yourself who holds the starring role here, and I'll give you one guess. Before you make your selection, however, here's a hint. It's already a given that the featured feline is a male based on pronoun usage, but it wasn't a Bausman. Any thoughts? Toss out a name, and then hit the footnotes[1].

Oh, potty training. You necessary beast, you. You necessary, sweat-inducing, energy-wringing beast. When it comes to toddlers, potty training is one of those things that parents simultaneously super-want and super-don't. It's awesome and it's longed for and it simplifies things ultimately…but it takes a crap-ton of effort and SO complicates life while it's underway. Potty training mastery is gold. The getting there part, though? Oiy. Potty training, you see, is both a prize and a penalty.

On the prize side of things, saying an indefinite farewell to diapers results in two major pluses, the first of which is cost savings. Arguably the most obvious benefit of potty training is the dough it restores to skinny wallets. Be they cloth or be they 'whatever that stuff is that takes 2000 years to biodegrade'[2], diapers are stupid expensive. When we were still a diaper-donning household, diapers were costly enough in and of themselves for Jonathan and me to have a designated diaper budget. It's kind of silly, really, that something with such a temporary and basic purpose costs what it does. OK, OK...perhaps on an individual level a single diaper isn't worth much, but diaper after diaper after diaper and day after day after day? It sure adds up quickly.

The other major plus of potty training victory? Dry heave savings. Yep, you heard me. Dry. Heave. Savings. Poop in all forms is gross, don't get me wrong, but there are simply grades of poop nastiness. On a level of one to ten, infant poop is like a one. It's ever-existing and it can be projectile (thanks, Annie!), but for the most part it's pretty tolerable. Before solids are introduced, infant poop hardly even smells...especially when it's breast milk generated. The solely breast milk stuff smells *sweet* at times, actually. Infant poop just isn't horrible. You know what *is* horrible, though? Like 'I'd take 100 infant diapers over this' horrible? Toddler poop. It's so, so gross and so, so pungent. Toddler tushies may retain some of their infantile cuteness, but what comes out of them is very different than those newborn days. More than once, toddler poop brought me to a place of losing my appetite and nearly losing my lunch, which is an impressive feat[3].

It was the idea of sparing myself another gag-worthy diaper change that led me to potty training Clark in the first place, honestly. I had recently transitioned from working part-time to staying at home full-time and had added on the commitment of providing childcare for Madison most days. Between Madison and Clark, who were about three months short of three years old, and Annie, who had just turned one, I felt like all I was doing was changing diapers. From sunup to sundown it was a poop and pee merry-go-round that never stopped spinning. One day, the three amigos must've done some behind the scenes planning because OH MAN did they come at me hard and heavy. I'm not even sure how it's possible with healthy, normal acting children in a span of only eight-ish hours, but I think the poop diaper tally was somewhere in the double digits. I called a 'code brown', texted my husband, and informed him that Potty Boot Camp was starting the next morning. I was so, super done with poop in multipliers of three.

Clark has always been an extremely bright and intelligent guy, but he never had interest in using the toilet. As is the case in nearly every other situation in life, if it's not Clark's idea, it's simply not an idea worth having. Clark didn't care if his diaper was wet, Clark didn't care if underwear in fun prints were dangled in front of his face, and Clark didn't care if chocolate awaited him in the event of potty victory. In Clark's analytical mind, he was most likely performing risk-reward assessments and determining that potty training, at the time anyway, just didn't offer him enough as compared to what it would cost. I can totally hear the internal conversation:

> **So, you're telling me that I'm going to have to slow down and halt play time on a regular basis throughout the day all for one or two measly M&M's and a monster truck on my butt? Nah— I'm good.**

For as long as my nose and stomach could tolerate it, we didn't push potty training with Clark. We let him call the shots on it, and we planned to let him tell us when he was ready…until Poop Fest 2017, that is. After that long, poop-filled day, I just couldn't get myself in the mental space I needed to be in in order to cheerfully change diaper after diaper after diaper after diaper (and so on…), especially when I knew that Clark was physically capable and, apart from his apathy and stubbornness, ready.

Because he really was ready—even if he wasn't exactly thrilled or even altogether willing to comply—potty training with Clark was mostly a breeze. *Clark* and *breeze* don't often go together in sentences where the latter takes on a meaning other than 'a gentle wind', so obviously Jonathan and I were thrilled that the process went the way it did for our guy. I followed through on my decision, Potty Boot Camp was initiated for both Clark and Madison, and we never looked back. In the beginning, boot camp was a hilarious variety show featuring toddlers nude from the waist down and plastic potties here, there, and everywhere. Boot camp was constantly responding to sounding timers, potty visit after potty visit, and endless and exorbitant praise. It was also tending to puddles of urine on the carpet, reassuring tearful (Madison) and frustrated (Clark) tots, and endless toddler potty scrubbing…but it worked, and the end result certainly justified the means it took to get there.

Potty training with Annie, on the other hand, is not what I would consider breezy. Because she saw big brother and big cousin using the potty for most of her little life, Annie wanted in…early. Like before she was even two years old early. I know that some of you are probably thinking that early potty training sounds like a blessing and a gift, and yes it is—eventually—but my first reaction to Annie's interests was not an "*Oh, yes!*". It was an "*Oh, NO!*" Clark was physically very ready for potty training, but Jonathan and I had to light a fuse under his behind to make it happen. Annie was physically very *not* ready for potty training. Jonathan and I drug our feet a little, if I'm being honest, but our girl wanted it, and she wasn't taking no for an answer. It was kind of like a repeat of the crib days. Clark was complacent and would have ridden out diaper-wearing indefinitely. On the flip side, Annie mandated freedom she wasn't ready for. While I can count on my hands the amount of times that Clark has had an accident of any sort and can confidently say that he has never,

ever-ever pooped anywhere other than a potty since we gave diapers the boot, Annie continues to require quite a good bit of encouragement and reminding a year into the process. She's a champ overall and far surpassed the expectations I had for potty training the second time around—don't mishear me—but potty training with Annie has simply been a lot more typical and a lot less dreamy than it was with an older, readier Clark.

Regardless of how ready or unready the trainee may be, potty training requires a lot of consideration, decision-making, and elbow grease on the part of the trainer. It poses questions such as:

-What type of training potty are we going to use?

-Where are we going to keep the potty/potties we are using?

AND

-What form of bribery will best engage our child?

Making a selection on training potties is overwhelming. You can go deluxe, and select varieties that sing songs, shout cheers of congratulations, and even light up when a wee one wees. At the other end of the spectrum, you can go basic and opt out of any added gadgets altogether. No matter what is selected, however, there is room for complication. The standalone potties are adorable and fun, but they are a bugger to clean…especially when potty breaks are happening practically every 15 minutes initially. Let me just tell you, the toddler poop that sits in those cute, musical potties is not made any more magical or less disgusting even with added bells and whistles. The toilet seat toppers? Well, they're fun too and are a perfect fit for little hineys…but a lot of times they leave just the right amount of space for a gross ring of pee to collect and crystallize. Jonathan, especially, finds them annoying. And how about going au naturel? While using the regular old toilet seat is definitely doable with adult help, both of my children have fallen in the toilet even *with* my help a time or two and have somehow managed to squirt pee down the front of the toilet instead of into the toilet a good dozen or more times without the use of kid-friendly attachments. Nothing comes easy, I suppose.

If you're like me, having just one toddler potty or even just one method of toddler potty-ing doesn't even come close to cutting it. Oh, no. When we were deep in the days of toilet training, we had like a solid five standalone units along with a seat topper. Potties, potties, everywhere. The funniest part of it all is that you guys know me well enough by now. I'm an anti-stuff girl and a less-is-more girl. But I'm also a gotta-be-prepared girl and a control-what-I-can girl. What did this mean for a bunch of potty training Bausmans? Well, because *"I gotta go!"* sometimes translates to *"I'm already going!"*, we were well stocked on potty preparations…especially on the road.

No one appreciates how very disgusting public restrooms are quite like toddler parents. You know how even the cleanest-looking of common toilets give you the skeevies and make you want to wash your hands a little while longer? Try keeping down your lunch while your toddler peeks into the sanitary receptacle, places her bare hands on the visibly soiled underside of the toilet seat, or (yup) proceeds to sit on the floor of the stall and put her shoe in her mouth. How Annie hasn't succumbed yet to dysentery, I simply have no clue. Because public restrooms are gross and I have even grosser toddlers, I avoid them like the plague if I can. Today, this is much simpler as unlike myself who possesses a bladder the size of a pea (very intentional word choice there, by the way), both of my kids can put down fluids and hold onto them like a camel. When potty training was new, however, we needed to be ready for unexpected needs always. For this reason, Ashley will forever be my savior.

Just like me, Ash had quite a collection of tot pots strewn all around her home in the days of potty training. Additionally, however, she was the Jedi master of preparedness and kept one in each of her vehicles. When Jonathan and I started our attempts with Clark, Ash made sure to recommend that we do the same. In the land of toddlers, this was probably the most valuable of nuggets I've ever received. It's a toddler life hack. So much so that had Alicia and Joe done the same initially, I would have had to use a different story to open this chapter. I bet you can guess where the yard sale acquired potty was stashed after our trip to the fair. The car trunk. I can't tell you how many times our trunk-appointed potty has made itself useful and saved us public restroom visits or accidents in hard-to-clean car seats. Today, for example, it kept my sweet Annie from using what I would argue is even fouler than most public bathrooms: the porta-john.

So you've picked your potty and you're as prepared as you can be both at home and on the road. Now what? Now, you select your bribery. As a word, 'bribery' may have a negative connotation or a bad reputation, but it really is an effective tool. If you like to use terms that are more feel-good in nature, stick with 'reward'…but I call things like they are. I have been bribing my children for as long as they were bribable and you know what? It works! Who doesn't work harder or try a little longer when they know their efforts will pay off? Be it stickers, or money[5], or a piece of chocolate, using the potty is just a little more appealing when bribery is involved.

Like their momma, my children happen to be fairly food motivated. While initially our system of one M&M for a #1 and two M&M's for a #2 wasn't enough to get Clark to cross the line from diapers to underwear on his own, it was enough to keep him interested once we made that decision for him. Although Annie was super on board at first and was the one who forced our hands into entering the potty training days yet again, she kind of reneged a few days later when she realized that being a 'big kid' meant putting play time aside for potty usage on a regular basis. At that point, however, we saw what she was capable of and had already put a lot of the hardest work in, so we persisted, and thankfully our girl loves herself some M&M's. To this day, both Clark and Annie will occasionally request a piece of candy when they use the bathroom and it just kind of makes me laugh that they're conditioned this way. When I think it over for a minute, shrug my shoulders, and say "*Sure!*", it's probably not the best execution of my parenting skills. Cooperation and listening aren't the strongest character traits of either of my two, however, so sometimes I choose to reward such behavior…even with sugar.

Potty training is just one of those parts of toddlerhood that is necessary, and inevitable, and unavoidable. When 'training' is a part of the title, there really should be no surprise that effort lies ahead. When has training for anything ever been pure fun or bliss? Think about it. People train for marathons. They train for new jobs. They weight train. They train to administer CPR. They train disobedient pets. At its core, training is a process. It requires instruction, it requires practice, and it requires follow-through. Because of this, the reality is that more than likely, potty training a toddler—even an easy one—is going to involve a bit of struggle from time to time. There was (and is) struggle for me, of course, but here's the truth. When I look back over the experience of potty training as a whole with both Clark and with Annie, I can honestly say that for all of the effort it required of Jonathan and me, I remember a lot more of the pride and the accomplishment and the celebration than I do of the setbacks. I remember the high fives. I remember the cheers. I remember the first drop of pee in a pot and—yes, I'm going there—the first, properly placed, tiny turd. I remember tears of joy. I remember the looks of excitement on my children's faces. I remember the congratulatory M&M's, and Tootsie Rolls, and ice cream cones (I'm telling you…we Bausmans speak food). I remember cancelling the diaper subscription. I remember the first day and then week and then month that poop landed nowhere other than a toilet. Happy days, guys, happy days.

This chapter, truthfully, was a bit of a challenge for me. For as buzz worthy of a topic as potty training is in the world of toddlers and for as much material as I did, ultimately, pull together to share with you…it took a lot of mental searching to piece together snippets of something that I look upon more with favor than I do with frustration. I'm glad to report that on this front specifically, it is easier for me to recall our victories than it is our failures. I don't want you to incorrectly hear what I am saying and think that I'm trying to paint inaccurate pictures because believe me, there was (and still is) strife in the potty world, but potty training has served me well.

Potty training, you see, is a balance of demand and delivery. For everything that it requires of you, it gives something back. It requires planning, and time, and energy, and willpower, and persistence, but it gives you far more money, far less dry heaves, and a whole-whole-lotta wins. Yes, there will be accidents. Yes, there will be unexpected pit stops during road trips. And, yes, there will be moments of *"This is why Mommy asked you to use the bathroom five minutes ago!"* But there will also be maturation. There will also be growth. And…there will also be obvious and almost-instantaneous fruit in a world where gains are often much, much more on the long-term level. I'm no potty training expert, and I'm sure I've done a number of things 'wrong' according to the pros when it comes to how I taught my kiddos to squat on a pot, but if potty training is a match to be won… I'd say Jonathan and I have nearly arrived at checkmate. Toilet *paper* training, though, now that's a different story[6]…

Footnotes

[1] Of course, it was Tristan!

[2] No judgment from me on this one (or ever!) guys. I'm one of *those* people…the disposable diaper people. If I have solar panels on my roof, which I surely do, does this negate the harm I've caused the environment or make me any less terrible of a person? Here's to hoping!

[3] I have a stomach of steel. While many things in life make me say "Eww!" and I can pass out basically on command[4] it takes a whole lot to actually bring me to a place of tossing my figurative cookies. I experienced nausea 24 hours a day for the first 16 weeks of both of my pregnancies, but never once did I actually 'get sick'. I wanted to, believe me, and I even tried to force it a time or two hoping for relief, but my gag reflex is insurmountable. I recognize that the moment I type this I am going to be stricken with a stomach virus straight from the pits of Hell, but I haven't graced a toilet with the contents of my stomach for more

than ten years. How do I know an exact number, you ask? Well, because the last time I was ill this way was on my honeymoon, when my dear and very-new husband served me undercooked chicken and gave me food poisoning. My insides were in agony, and I passed out…on the toilet…naked. Jonathan panicked, called 911, and then proceeded to have a good chat about the IT world with the security guard who showed up in our hotel room before the medics did. All while I lay in a semi-conscious state of misery. Oh my goodness is this hilarious now, but it maybe wasn't so much when I was living it.

[4] My apologies for the reference within a reference, but I just have to say at this point that I have no idea how I ever functioned as a nurse. I can care for my children and handle any yuck they throw at me, but honest-to-goodness if I look at myself in the mirror the wrong way or spot blood on Jonathan, it's game over. Ha!

[5] My mom chose to utilize bribery in the form of money with my sisters and me when we potty trained. Her line of thinking was that it was a healthier and more readily-available alternative to candy…and boy did it backfire. Once, my mom gave me a nickel after I achieved success on the toilet and then proceeded to lay me down on the floor in order to put my pants back on. As I held up my nickel to admire it, it dropped. Down my throat. One phone call to the pediatrician, one visit to the emergency room, and one x-ray later showed that the nickel was safely housed in my small intestine and had not caused any sort of obstruction. The nickel would simply have to pass, which it did. My poor grandmother, who provided childcare for me at the time, had to literally sift through my diapers for treasure. Treasure which remains taped to a page of my baby book to this day, in fact. Oh, and this is also the same mother who helped me gather poison ivy for my preschool leaf collection. That was a fun week of my life. Love you, Ma!

[6] If there are any seasoned parents out there who want to throw down some advice on toilet paper usage and wiping one's own bottom, I'm game to listen. Clark is currently on the learning curve in this regard and uses about 15 disposable wipes at every go. Our poor pipes.

9 FOOD FUN

In the Bausman household, we believe in balance.

-A balance of **power**. As in, sometimes I rule my children, and sometimes they rule me.

-A balance of **practicality**. As in, every day Jonathan drives a Toyota Yaris, but for one day, he and I rented a Porsche (It was a business trip in Vegas. We made it fun.)

-A balance of **rigidity**. As in, some days it's "No, you may not have your Kindle. Let's play hide and go seek together…" while other days it's "Another three episodes of Tumble Leaf? Absolutely."

-A balance of **spending**. As in, I can purchase an entire week's worth of groceries for less than 75 dollars if I try to, yet I maybe spent over eight dollars on a solitary macchiato last week (also in Vegas—where everything is stupid expensive—so I'm going to say I get a pass on this one…)

AND

-A balance of **nutrition**. As in, some mornings, my children eat homemade, whole-wheat pancakes that are shaped like X's, O's, and hearts, and some mornings, they eat cold pizza.

My toddlers have very much eaten cold pizza for breakfast[1]. They've also eaten donuts for dinner and super recently (as in *today*), icing-coated muffins for lunch. For as much as it may not seem like it given the last two sentences you've read, I really and truly do care how my children's bodies are nourished and put forth effort to make sure that their diet is colorful, natural, and broad. My kids are not just chicken nugget and hot dog kids. Not all of the time, anyway. They are also salmon kids. They are quinoa kids. They are edamame kids. They are chia-and-flaxseed-in-everything-Mommy-bakes kids.

Keeping toddlers fed is a balancing act, you see. A non-stop, always-changing, labor-intensive balancing act. It's a few parts organic, but one part processed. It's a few parts elbow grease, but one part convenience. It's a few parts insisting, but one part relenting. And, it's a few parts success, and one part—just kidding...a LOT of parts—failure. Most of the time, I make meal selections that are well-rounded and tickle the taste buds, but with toddlers in the picture, there are simply other times when what lands on our plates is the product of being rushed, flat-out fatigued, or dictated over.

When it comes to food, toddlers have gobs of opinions. Strong, pointed, unfiltered opinions. They have immature, narrow-minded palates, they're stubborn, they are creatures of habit and routine, and they don't typically love to do things that may even potentially cause them discomfort...all of which often rolls over into less-than-adventurous eating. If a toddler likes cheese crackers shaped like a certain aquatic animal, chances are he's going to stick with those beloved finned friends. If a toddler doesn't think he is going to like something, chances are he's not even going there.

Before I had toddlers of my own, I must admit that I cast some judgement on this topic as a whole. I assumed that the things these tiny tots put into their mouths was directly a result of parental mindfulness and effort. My line of thinking was this: *If your child only eats mac and cheese, it's because you let him eat only mac and cheese. Give him a tomato. Tell him to eat the tomato. He will like the tomato.*

Oh, Whitney. You were downright silly to think that toddlers— and taste buds, for that matter—are so malleable, adaptive, and easy to control. Nowadays, while I won't concede that it's impossible to develop toddler tastes and encourage an interest in more than a handful of kid staples, I've also witnessed with my own eyes the willpower of a stubborn tyke or two.

Today, I'm on the receiving end of toddler tyranny. I so understand the concept of choosing one's battles and keeping the peace when it is possible to do so. Because of this, when a parent informs me that their kiddo's daily intake consists of fruit snacks and Oreos, I don't cringe, I don't judge, and I don't offer suggestions that have worked for my own two. I just get it. If not fighting food battles means tons less fighting altogether, I so-so get it.

On the spectrum of daring diners as related to toddlers, I've kind of struck gold. Yes, of course, there are things my children refuse to put in their mouths[2], but if you hand either Clark or Annie a kale salad topped with feta cheese and olives, I can guarantee you that they will put it down. Happily. While I'd like to think that some of this food-related boldness comes as a result of me continually introducing and re-introducing foods to my children and providing them the same dinner that I am providing to my hubby and me the majority of the time, I fully recognize that some of these tendencies aren't learned. Another parent doing all of the same things that I do may have a toddler whose jaws only open for processed, white carbohydrates. In some cases, I really do think that pickiness or choosiness is innate. Or at least partially[3].

While my kids have always been the bread crust and apple peel eating variety and are fairly easy to please when it comes to food, they are what I would consider *selectively* picky. For starters, they often exhibit a behavior that is core to toddler eating. For days on end, Clark and Annie have little interest in taking time out from play to stop and put anything of substance in their mouths. Unless I toss them a super-processed cookie or something equally awful that they can eat on the run, it seems they don't really eat. Days later, however, the pendulum swings and my refrigerator isn't large enough to house all of the food required to satiate their ravenous appetites. On these days, they are always hungry, will eat whatever I lay before them, and come up searching for more.

Selective pickiness also rears its head in the form of rotating likes and dislikes under our roof. In the span of a day, it is very possible for either Clark or Annie to go from loving something to hating something or vice versa. I dub this 'the novelty concept'. For example, if my kids haven't had grapes for several days, when they catch sight of them, those grapes are inhaled. If, however, I take note that they really enjoyed their grapes for lunch today and, thusly, serve them grapes again for lunch tomorrow…those very same grapes will sit on the plate untouched. When a food is novel or new or rediscovered after a hiatus worth noting, Clark and Annie dive in. They only dive in for one meal, however. As soon as a food is enjoyed, it becomes old news and has to go back into the rotation.

When foods aren't adequately rotated per Clark and Annie's demands, there is an unfortunate and frustrating amount of food waste in my home. For Jonathan and me personally, food waste is one of our biggest pet peeves as parents, and it's tough for us to swallow. We try to be ultra-conscious of portion size and provide our kids only with what we think they will actually ingest, but honestly, we could put a single peanut on their plates some days and it would go uneaten. Because we can't stand tossing perfectly good food away, Clark and Annie's food waste often leads Jonathan and me to serving as human garbage disposals. With regularity, Jonathan and I ingest more calories and more toddler-touched, germy food remnants than we would ideally like to. How we aren't constantly reaching for a box of tissues…I'm just not sure.

Food waste and toddlers are synonymous, and, for a number of reasons, this makes me crazy. Firstly, I have personally witnessed starvation and malnutrition both globally and locally. In my own experience as a school nurse, my heart has broken for and my efforts have gone into providing resources for children who have returned to school on a Monday morning with aching, hollow bellies that weren't filled over the weekend. It's hard for me to toss food into the trash can that I know others long for, dream of, and truly-truly *need*. Secondly, and far less importantly, food waste makes me crazy because while my toddlers will report that they are just "too full" to eat what's on their plates, they are the same toddlers who are begging for candy or ice cream or some other sugar-filled wonder five minutes later. Thirdly, food waste makes me crazy because of the *effort* that is thrown in the garbage right alongside the scraps.

We've talked extensively about servanthood already, but food-related servanthood is simply on a whole other level. Unlike bathing which can go a day or two (or four…) without much of a consequence, laundering dirty clothes which could go a week or more, or picking up of messes which really won't cause the world to implode should they be ignored, keeping a child fed is different. Keeping a child fed is legally and instrumentally required. Keeping a child fed is necessary…lots of times a day. Feeding toddlers (or any children for that matter) is a constant loop of food preparation, food service, and food cleanup. Even minimally demanding snacks and meals somehow seem to take effort, but add in even a speck of creativity, the use of fresh ingredients, or anything that isn't 100% instant? You know, toddler-friendly stuff like color-themed meals, cute-shaped sandwiches, and plates featuring items that little hands helped choose carefully from that week's crop share? Oh man, these things take time and effort.

Being a toddler parent cracks me up when it comes to what is done for others versus what is done for self in the realm of food. I've said already that I prepare the same dinnertime meal for my children that I prepare for myself and for Jonathan, and that is 100% true. The same cannot be said for breakfast and lunch, though. I do cut corners often and tend to go for tried-and-true, lazy staples like whole grain waffles, yogurt, and 'snack plates'[4], but on the days I watch Madison, I plan and prepare things that partner nutrition, variation, and fun.

Not always, but often, the more 'fun' things also happen to be more time consuming. On any given week day, it isn't uncommon for me to pour myself into making some recipe I've stumbled upon or invented myself for a solid 30 minutes or more only to hand off plates to uninterested palates. Sometimes—who am I kidding...*often* times—these handoffs are thankless, cleanup commences only moments later, and after an hour or so I realize that I, myself, never ate lunch. Do I invest another 30 minutes or even another five minutes into making something for me? Nah. I grab a cheese stick and an apple and call it a win because I am either A: too tired, or B: on to the next task, which is usually cleaning up the food now coating the table and floor. I swear that at least half of the sustenance I give my toddlers ends up on their faces, their clothing, or their surroundings. I really don't know how they continue to grow when they consume so little of what is provided them.

Despite the fact that my children oftentimes eat only a portion of what they are given, give me an "EWWWWW" after I've tried my best to choose a recipe I thought they would enjoy, or beg to be freed from the table about two bites after they sit down, they will also, ironically, cling to my legs and plead to be fed while I am preparing the dinner they will ultimately diss some nights. Do you remember the complicated process I spoke of a few chapters back where I mentioned having to hunt down my children and essentially carry them to the table at meal times? Well, while this is a very accurate depiction of life in my home when my toddlers are in one of their 'play always-eat never' hunger strikes, it is very much not the case when they are on the opposite end of the cycle. When my kids are *really* hungry, I can't get them off of me. Hanger, it turns out, is real[5]. Just like their momma, when my kids need fuel, they're cranky and they let you know it.

On hanger nights, the 30 minutes before dinner is ready are torture for everyone involved. I'm hungry, so I'm sassy, and my kids are hungry, so they're evil. Basically it's "I scream, you scream, we all scream for ice cream…" except without any of the lightheartedness and with a lot more hostility. I'm convinced that even the sanest and absolute best of toddler parents approach the brink of criminality occasionally in these tense moments before dinner bells ring. Once, to save myself from such crimes, I absolutely plopped a still crib-bound Annie in her figurative jail cell along with her brother, threw them a Kindle, and told Clark I'd give him chocolate after dinner if he 'babysat' for me while I got our meal together. Real life, guys. Real life.

Whether it's trying to tame these rabid cats when they are hungry or trying to coax them to eat more than a bite of something of quality when they're ultra-willing to nosh on junk, food battles in Toddler Land are evident, exhausting, and pretty darn common. Food-related emergencies in my household? Oh, those are pretty common too. While neither of my kiddos have any food intolerances that we are aware of (which I am incredibly grateful for both as a school nurse and as a friend to individuals with profound allergies), we have had our fair share of medical scares when it comes to things that are edible.

On one end of the spectrum are the minor scares. Some examples of our minor scare occurrences would be the handful of times that either or both of my children have crammed tiny foods like peas and peanuts into their nostrils and ears. These events are those that are enough to give me momentary concern, but are easily remedied and require no further intervention…other than reminders (for the 700th time) that food doesn't belong in holes on our heads apart from the mouth, of course. And then, there are the mid-level scares. The mid-level scare that jumps into my brain right now would be the time that a less-than-two-year-old Annie discovered that she could open the refrigerator, crammed a handful of whole grapes into her mouth chipmunk style, and then proceeded to choke on them. Thank God she was OK and somehow didn't even need the Heimlich maneuver from me, but mid-level scares do require intervention. In this case? Jonathan and I applied a toilet lock on the refrigerator. In fact, it's still there even today so that Mommy gets to determine when and what Annie eats and drinks. The girl is a scavenger.

Lastly, we arrive at our major scares. To the best of my recollection, there has only been one food-related major scare in our home, but it's quite an elaborate one. Remember how I said that I struck gold on adventurous-eating toddlers? Well, it's true. Maybe too true. My children request sushi more often than I do, they are hot tea enthusiasts, and apparently, they are also foragers.

Two summers ago, Jonathan and I were watching Ashley and her husband Kyle's four boys for the weekend. We were in the back yard playing, when I noticed Clark running towards me with a big smile plastered on his face and a mouth full of *something*.

CLARK: Mommy, guess what! I ate a healthy food. I ate a mushroom!

ME: You ate a what, bud?

CLARK: I ate a mushroom!

ME: Where did you get a mushroom?

CLARK: Right there! (points behind him, towards the grass)

ME: Spit it out NOW, Clark. Spit it out, spit it out, spit it out!

Caught off guard and confused as to why his nutritious ambition had been negatively received by Mommy, Clark's eyes were instantly filled with tears as I scooped him up and hurried to find Jonathan. I spotted my husband, reported what had happened, and asked that he please rinse Clark's mouth as best as possible and give the doctor a quick phone call just to make sure that we didn't need to do anything further.

I was a smidge anxious only because I knew that mushrooms have the potential to be harmful, but I wasn't overly concerned as Clark had spit out most of what was left in his mouth. When I was updated moments later by my man, however, I wasn't quite so put-together. As soon as the nurse on the pediatrician's triage line heard the word 'mushroom', she connected Jonathan to Poison Control. From there, we were given instructions on monitoring breathing and assessing for other signs of toxicity for a full 36 hours. Even though Clark was completely asymptomatic and our knowledgeable-about-all-things-nature friend, Bryan, was fairly certain our guy's appetizer was an edible variety of fungus, we were even instructed to wake Clark overnight to ensure that he was demonstrating no difficulty in breathing. The folks from Poison Control called and checked in on us every few hours through the following day. They were amazing, reassuring, and so helpful. Thankfully, Clark was totally fine and Bryan's identification of the culprit as a 'fairy ring' was spot on. Never a dull moment over here. Never a dull moment.

Regardless of whether they are frustrating or time-consuming or hilarious or scary or successful or exhausting or gratifying, food matters with toddlers are simply inescapable. By nature, toddlers must eat to survive. Also by nature, toddlers are self-centered and self-protective. What does this mean? Well, in the mind of a toddler, eating isn't about survival. It's about comfort. It's about eating foods they like. It's about avoiding foods they don't. It's about finding what tastes most satisfying and sticking with it. Because toddlers' concern is self-first and self-highest, they want what they perceive is best for them when they perceive it best for them and they just don't want it any other way. So when Clark's idea of a good dinner is the giant brownie topped with chocolate frosting that he's had his eye on all afternoon, he may not be a willing or happy consumer when Mommy plops grilled chicken and southwest salad down in front of him. Or, when Annie demands that it's time to eat—again—even though she just had breakfast an hour ago and a snack after that? "No" is not an option. Or at least it's not an option if Mommy would rather have any shot at being productive than lugging around a thirty pound weight that has affixed itself to her ankles. A *screaming* thirty pound weight, no less.

Toddlers have opinions on food, they have preferences with food, and they have all-out meltdowns over food. Sometimes, there are just stubborn and steadfast wills to overcome. Sometimes, there are true texture issues, swallowing concerns, or food anxieties to overcome. Sometimes, there are narrow minds to overcome. Sometimes, there is sheer hanger to overcome. No matter the toddler, it seems, there will be food hurdles along the way. As long as toddlers continue needing food to function, cat herders will be fighting food battles.

In my home, food battles are one of the most consistent areas of struggle that Jonathan and I face on a daily basis…and this is with a pair of toddlers who are most definitely foodies in the making. We're talking about the duo who was spotted eating Korean bulgogi bao in the not so distant past. The problem, though, is that regardless of how broad their palates are becoming, Clark and Annie are still toddlers at the core. A lot of times, the snacks and meals that find themselves in front of those palates are selected without their direct input, and as we've already established…my toddlers only like to entertain ideas that are their own. Always. So, while it is true that my children may have happily eaten bao one day when the stars aligned, they were actually hungry, and what they saw looked appealing enough to insight intrigue, it is also true that these very same children were spotted eating a ghastly 'breakfast' of plain, sliced, untoasted, awful-awful for you, white bread a few weeks back. Why, you ask? Because on that day, I had other battles to fight.

When you're living with and caring for toddlers, the un-fun version of food fights just happen. They happen at home, they happen in restaurants[6], and they happen in the grocery store. While these moments are oh-so-exasperating and seem to repeat themselves on a loop without end, it's the other sort of food moments that keep me going. The fewer and further between, but super-awesome, moments. Like when Clark got to take a packed lunch to preschool for the first time ever a few months ago and I gave him the reins. His selections? Veggie couscous salad, shelled edamame, bell pepper strips, and one modest piece of chocolate. My heart was dancing. Or when my children, in tandem, decided to leave Santa black coffee this year instead of milk because they've grown to love its magic as much as Daddy and I do[7]. Proud, proud parents.

I am the first one to admit that there are days when I invest way too much time in crafting plates I *think* my children will enjoy. For every ten attempts at a 'fun' food, I would estimate that maybe one or two results in any sort of excitement on the part of my toddlers. You know what, though, I'll take it. The one in ten positive reaction—the one with squeals of joy and maybe even the elusive "thank you"—makes even the failed attempts worthwhile. For as many calories as I burn in trudging my way through the food battles of toddlerhood and for as much as I super-want to throw in the towel some days and pretend like a popcorn and ice cream dinner was pre-planned, I will continue to hold my head up high and believe that I'm really doing OK on the whole food front. Yes, my children eat and give two thumbs WAY up to junk in all forms, but as long as these things are the exception and not the rule, I'm good.

Remember the asthmatic cat I once owned? The one who I couldn't force to take medication that was inherently beneficial to him and good for him? Again I say…toddlers are cats. Try as I'd like, I can't really force my toddlers to do much of anything let alone chew and swallow a piece of zucchini. If you're currently in a place of nonstop madness when it comes to food and feel like your little one survives on either A: nothing, B: fish-shaped crackers or C: crap…take a deep breath, put your chin up, and carry on.

If you're feeling brave, try enlisting your little one(s) to 'help' in the kitchen. While Annie would rather play with her babies or enjoy a bit of screen time while I cook, Clark is all in when it comes to food prep. He's been my little sous chef for years, and we really do make a good team. Together, we've concocted reindeer cookies for his preschool classmates, droolworthy salads, the fluffiest of pancakes, bangin' bowlfuls of homemade chicken pot pie[8], and marshmallow rice treats that folks go gaga over (thanks for the tips, Doug!). Cooking with toddlers may be messy and require a little extra patience and time, but in my home at least, Clark and Annie are a whole lot more likely to try something new for me if their hands helped to either select it or prepare it.

When it comes to partnering food and toddlers, do what you *can* do—things like introducing healthy foods again and again and again and again, rewarding and praising new attempts out the wazoo, and modeling the food behaviors you expect your little ones to demonstrate themselves[9]—and dust the rest off of your shoulders. Eventually, these toddlers will eat more than a handful of carb-laden foods. Eventually, these toddlers will sit still for longer than three seconds at a time…maybe even long enough to last for an entire meal. Eventually, these toddlers will turn into parents with their own toddlers and fight the same fights. And believe you me, guys…I'll be looking through the window LAUGHING.

Footnotes

[1] For the record, Daddy was in charge that morning. I just happened to think his menu selection was awesome.

[2] The things my toddlers don't like crack me up, actually. Annie will eat truly spicy food like it's no big deal, but the boxed mac and cheese that children typically go nuts over is blasé in her world. Oh, and speaking of cheese…Clark hates the stuff. In certain forms, anyway. You can give Clark feta or parm any day of the week, but plain-jane cheddar or

mozzarella? Criminal. Clark doesn't even eat cheese on pizza, yet he will pound beets like they're going out of style. Weirdo.

[3] Scientists today are actually linking strong food preferences to genetic markers.

[4] 'Snack plates' are a combination of healthy-ish, prep-free bites like nuts, grapes, raisins, and granola…or basically whatever I can readily grab from my pantry or refrigerator, plop on a plate, and say "Voilà!" to.

[5] In case you aren't up on modern lingo. Hunger + Anger = Hanger.

[6] Sometimes, it feels like toddlers and restaurants go together like water and oil. Dining out with children in the picture is just different. It requires a lot of distraction, a lot of bribery, and a lot of ordering whatever will be prepared the quickest and most-easily inhaled. These days, Jonathan and I are much more the 'mobile order and go' sort.

[7] Is this not the most sensible thing you've ever heard? Milk, in a warmed form anyway, is used to induce sleepiness. Why on Earth would Santa want to drink something repeatedly that's going to weigh him down and give him the nods? Santa clearly wants coffee, people. Take it from Clark and Annie.

[8] When you live in Pennsylvania Dutch Country, chicken pot pie is most definitely served in a bowl…and no crust is involved.

[9] There's nothing worse than when I come down hard on Clark for turning his nose up at something on his plate before he even tastes it and then have to listen to Jonathan's laughter and snide remarks when he offers me a bite of something he brought home from work and I give that suggestion a big old N-O.

10 "VACATION"

Welcome to the chapter pertaining to all things 'vacation'. All things 'vacation'…as it relates to toddlers, that is. We're talking beach trips, amusement parks, mountain retreats, and museums. We're talking travel by land, by air, and by sea. The fun stuff. The thrilling stuff. The *exhausting* stuff. Wait a second…exhausting?! Aren't vacations, by nature, supposed to be relaxing or at least exhilarating? Aren't vacations supposed to fill you more than they drain you? If you look up 'vacation' as a term, you'll find common descriptions featuring words such as leisure, unwinding, travel, pleasure, and 'doing what you want'. Feel good words. Pick-me-up words. Take me away words. With toddlers in the picture, however? Well, I'm going to go out on a limb and say that vacations involving toddlers are just slightly different than the kid-free variety. And when I say slightly…clearly it's Opposite Day.

Vacations with toddlers are work. Vacations with toddlers are stressful. Vacations with toddlers are mental, physical, and emotional exercise. Why, then, do we bother? Well, because vacations with toddlers also provide excitement, new experiences, new surroundings, and the creation of beautiful memories. We want our children to see the world beyond the borders of their own community. We want them to put their hands in the sand if we are rural dwellers, the dirt if we are urban dwellers, and the snow if we are coastal dwellers.

Regardless of whether traveling from Point A to Point B involves one solo mean of transportation or a combination of many, the process of 'getting there' is complicated with little ones in the picture. Even the 'being there' part, however, is made different by their presence. Toddlers impact each and every part of vacationing, and I'd like to break this down point by point. Let's dive in!

Packing Up

Vacations start when bags are packed and cars are loaded. Before kids, this part of the process was a whole lot simpler, much more me-focused, and possible even in my always reliable, teeny-tiny Toyota Yaris. Add one tot? The story becomes, *"The SUV is full."* Add two? It's, *"What can we leave behind?"* Add three or four or even more? I think at that point the scenario is more likely, *"Who can we leave behind?"* Kidding, of course. But seriously, packing up with toddlers to consider is challenging.

When young children are in tow, you have to think about every possible angle of the trip before you even leave the comfort of your home. For starters, you have to think about what might be needed during travel. In this case, the list could include snacks, drinks, wipes, diapers/training pants/potty, a change of clothes, mess-free activities, comfort items like stuffed animals and blankets, and bribery in the form of sugar or a screen. Then, you have to think about what may be needed in the rented accommodations and the surrounding vicinities. In this regard, we're talking travel cribs, portable high chairs, toys, strollers, potty training supplies, monitors, white noise machines, sleeping companions, and bikes or bike seats. Finally, you have to think about what may be needed when 'vacation' is underway. If it's a beach trip, toddlers love inflatable pools and gobs of bulky sand toys and need life jacket vests, UV-protective clothing, collapsible beach wagons and pop-up tents. If it's an amusement park, we're talking ID bands in the event of separation, hats and sunglasses and sunscreen, and even the possibility of a toddler leash…which we'll revisit shortly. Regardless of the venue, packing with toddlers in mind always-always includes added stuff. LOTS of added stuff.

Traveling by Car

After each and every item from the pages-long packing list is gathered and secured, then comes the part of vacation that all toddler parents fear: *travel*. No matter the means, travel with toddlers is complicated, and cumbersome, and just plain daunting. So much thought and preparation have to go into ensuring that some form of either entertainment or bribery is at the ready every possible minute. Even short car rides with toddlers are exhausting and expert-level challenges in the multitasking department. Long rides, though? Like hours-long rides? Well, they require physical and mental stamina beyond what a parent possesses sometimes.

Long car rides with toddlers inevitably include demands. Long car rides with toddlers inevitably include potty breaks. Long car rides with toddlers inevitably include dropped cups, depleted snack supplies, spills, sibling battles, boredom, and pleas for freedom. In the earliest days of toddlerhood, pacifying an unhappy car rider just wasn't fun or easy. Why? Well, because these were the BC and BS days. Before candy and before screens, that is. Today, however, for as F- of a parent as it may make me, there are times in the car— especially when traveling long distances for vacation—when nothing short of a few gummy bears or a rousing 2,000 renditions of 'the ice cream song' can fix. For those of you out there with toddlers who, like me, are ultra-prone to motion sickness… I AM SO SORRY[1].

Traveling by Air

It's pretty obvious that riding in a car with a toddler entails a whole lot of challenges and obstacles. What happens, however, when travel doesn't end with a car? What happens, instead, when the car is only the beginning? Oh, hello, airplane. While airplane travel with children is in many ways awesome as it saves hours of time on the road, it also adds new hurdles and hoops to jump through. Example? Security. Getting through security is in and of itself a stressful and oftentimes slow process. Add in toddlers? Good gravy. Getting through security with toddlers is herding cats to the core. You've got to partially disrobe yourself, empty your pockets, dump the water or milk being stashed in sippy cups[2], fold and carry a clunky stroller, remove stowed electronics, properly position your property in bins, and then meander through a metal detector…all while trying to maintain possession of one or more uncooperative tots who would rather be doing anything other than being held or held onto. Fun times.

When you're traveling in the air with little ones, the ride has the potential to be so much worse than when traveling by car. SO much. First, if and when your toddler turns evil in the car, there are options for escape. While delaying arrival isn't ideal, pit stops can be made, captives can be set free to stretch their legs, and peace can be regained. In an airplane? Not happening. Further, if and when your toddler turns evil in the car, those directly impacted are other loved ones or at least folks who know what they are getting themselves into. In an airplane? Not exactly. In an airplane, not only are *you* held hostage to your toddler's antics and ear-piercing screams, but so are rows upon rows upon rows of strangers. Strangers who always seem to hate children, no less.

Airplane travel brings with it all of the necessities of car travel, but it goes far beyond them. When flying with Clark and Annie, I seriously feel like a bag lady with the most random assortment of items. We're talking magnets, post-it notes, tattoos, stickers, bandages, books, tape, mess-free markers, snacks enough for a week, and, of course, screens and sweets[3]. Basically *any*thing to distract little hands and minds.

In the realm of flying with toddlers, Jonathan and I have had some home runs and some strikeouts. On one hand, we have been pleasantly surprised by Clark, who tends to fall into a state of awe and amazement at the workings of the airplane and its staff. He becomes abnormally cooperative simply because he's in stimuli overdrive. Clark loves the mechanical side of everything, and an airplane is kind of his sweet spot. On the other hand, though, we have been flustered by Annie, whose disdain for restraint somehow seems to grow exponentially in the air.

A little over a year ago, Annie was Miserable with a capital M on a flight to 'the most magical place on Earth'. Our flight, however, was about the furthest thing from magical. It was almost laughable how very awful Miss Annie was[4]. For more than an hour, Annie was in a full tilt rampage because she wasn't being permitted to walk up and down the center aisle. She was tired, absolutely refused to nap, and would not accept bribery in any form. No matter the candy concoction or screen image we tried to placate her with, it was angrily tossed and only increased the volume of her screaming.

The best part of it all was Annie's drastic and unexplained turnaround. Just moments from landing, the screaming stopped, laughter returned, and a smile was plastered on her cute little face. I'm telling you…it was pixie dust. Without reason, our girl was sweet-as-pie, and she flirted with all of the strangers around her who she had just moments before been driving to the edge of their sanity. She knows how to work a crowd, this child. They were all under her spell in seconds. I even had Annie apologize to the poor people she terrorized during the flight, and it was done with flair. Grins, angelic eyes, and waves fitted for royalty. They were eating out of her hand, and I'm fairly certain the first 99% of the flight was forgotten…for the other passengers, anyway. Mommy and Daddy, though? We remember.

Personal Leisure

Before I had kids, vacations were leisurely, the pace was slow, and I did what I wanted to when I wanted to. If I felt motivated enough to head out for a run after breakfast or wanted to nap on the beach in the afternoon, so be it. Beach trips with toddlers in tow, though, look so much different. Now, because I don't want to abandon my husband to care for our two nor do I want to miss moments with my family, running either goes to the wayside or happens at stupid hours of the day like 5 AM[5]. And napping on my part? Ha! Nowadays, afternoon vacation hours look a lot more like me pushing a double stroller holding 60 plus pounds of toddler up and down a boardwalk for miles in hopes that one or both of my tired toddlers will cave to a brief rest.

With Clark and Annie in the picture, only a very small percentage of the things that take place during vacation have anything to do with Jonathan or me. Instead, we make decisions on where we stay based on our children. We make decisions on where we eat based on our children. We make decisions on how we spend our days based on our children. The things we do and the things we don't do are heavily, heavily influenced by the tykes we call our own.

Sleeping

When obtaining sleep is already a circus act at home, the circus only gets more rampant when on vacation. Away from home, there are unfamiliar beds, unfamiliar rooms, and atypical sleeping arrangements to overcome. All of this translates to a little extra TLC and coddling beyond the norm to help sleepy, little eyes succumb to slumber. And, without fail, there's always *something* that goes awry right about the time sleep is achieved. Like maybe a parade of 11 fully-clad firemen walking noisily through your vacation rental. Need I explain?

Jonathan, the kids, and I traveled to North Carolina with my mom and her husband, Tom, my Aunt Sharon, my sisters, their hubbies, and their tribe of children roughly 18 months ago. We rented one, mondo, beach house, and somehow managed to pull off a glorious week filled with laughter and cohesiveness despite the hurricane that rolled through the area. On one of our final nights together, the last of the 11 children had just gotten off to sleep, I was finally comfortable in bed with Jonathan, and together we were about to watch some television when the smoke detection system started blaring and flashing strobe lights throughout the entire house. Here's some honesty for you. A SMOKE alarm was sounding, and my first thoughts had absolutely nothing to do with safety or danger or the potential of fire. My first thoughts were, *"You've got to be kidding me. All of these kids are going to wake up."*

Somehow, and kind of frighteningly actually, not a single child popped up out of their beds or emerged from their rooms. When Jonathan and I did, however, we were greeted with the unpleasant aroma of something burning. Although we couldn't visualize flames anywhere and the sounding of the alarm ceased, this was no false alarm. Not *fully* false, anyway. As the other adults scattered throughout the vacation rental started appearing—each one sleepy-eyed and donning fabulous nighttime fashions—I phoned the property owner and contacted emergency services. Within minutes, the entire street was lit up with rescue vehicles and fire trucks, and nearly a dozen animated, hard-stepping firepersons with very little regard for sleeping children[6] were searching high and low for the source of the smell and the alarm triggerer.

We were advised to vacate the home until answers became clearer, but in stellar parent form, we all *begged* the emergency responders to let sleeping ~~dogs~~ cats lie. While those helping us weren't overly thrilled with the idea, they did agree not to wake any of the kids unless it was deemed necessary. The adults, however, they placed at the ready. The leader of the response team told us to get dressed, put on our shoes, and have our keys in our hands because, and I quote, *"If I tell you that you need to get out, I won't be asking twice."* He was kind of dramatic and kind of awesome.

By the grace of God, it was quickly discovered that an air handler in the attic space had overheated and had nearly set fire to the materials surrounding it. The responders were able to shut down the unit, spray coolant into the attic, and leave us in the same condition we were found within a matter of an hour or two. Oh, memories...

Safety

Toddlers pose a threat to themselves even at home. Whether it be Annie "just pretending" to put marbles in her mouth right after I witness her spit a solid three or four onto the carpet, or Clark placing a chair on the *stairs* to assist himself in turning on a light switch[7], these guys are destined for disaster. On vacation, though? Don't even get me started. Being in an unfamiliar setting is dangerous with toddlers simply because things are likely not child-proofed like they are at home. Exposed outlets. Sharp corners. That sort of stuff. When you add in the surroundings, however, and the potential hazards there...it's a lot to manage. At the beach, there is sand to ingest, the lure of open water, and unpredictable waves. In the mountains it's rocky terrain, steep cliffs, and itch-inducing plants. At an amusement park, it's the masses upon masses of people who pose a threat because for movers like my two, there is a true possibility of getting lost.

Never in my life have I been a kid-leash person...until I had Annie, that is. Ashley once gave me a leash backpack for Clark because she knew how crazy he was, but Jonathan and I never utilized it because it was always either a one-to-one or two-to-one situation in our favor. Yes, he was mobile from the start, but his mobility was manageable. With two nonstop tots, however, we met our match. Remember that less-than-magical airplane ride with Annie I spoke of? Well, the vacation that followed was slightly less-than-magical too. On top of battling teething, Annie saw fit to dash away from Jonathan and me any time we placed her feet on the ground yet would scream and fight the moment we picked her up. It was so exhausting. Did we take the leash along on that trip? Sadly, no. We were wrongly confident in ourselves and our cat taming abilities, so the leash stayed at home. Let me just say that had we taken it, Annie would have been leashed up big time.

Eating

Toddlers and food don't always go together nicely...we've already talked about this concept at length. Toddlers and food on vacation, though, well that can be even dicier. At home, toddlers may be picky and opinionated and stubborn when it comes to food, but at least there is somewhat of a routine and a sense of normalcy. On vacation, however, there are many more variables, new environments, and a real chance of basically every food rule going out the window. Hot donuts for breakfast? A visit to the ice cream truck at lunch? French fries, funnel cake, and fudge for dinner? Ehh, why not? Eating tends to be a little less natural and a lot more nostalgic beyond our own walls...and it also tends to be rushed. On a few occasions, Jonathan and I have been out with the kids while traveling, have stopped at a place with a great-looking menu, been super excited to order something new, and have then been forced to either inhale our food down or leave much of it uneaten as a result of toddlers who are simply *done* and who have reached their limit. Let's keep it real...other times, we've been prepared enough to shove lollipops in their mouths or hand over the dreaded screen simply for a few more minutes to properly chew our own dinners.

Day-to-Day Life

There's something to be said for the comfort and familiarity of one's own home. When you're an introvert, like me, this is especially true. In my own space, I know what my kids can and can't get into, I know what dangers exist, I am stocked with tons of age-appropriate entertainment, I've grown to accept that my toddlers make everything dirty and use everything *hard*, and I am very much used to all things LOUD. When I'm out of my element and occupying someone else's space, stability in a sense, is lost. I think this is why we toddler parents pack so much gosh darn stuff for our children when we travel. We want to be prepared for everything, and we want to have as much of a normal and typical day as we can even when we are away from home.

While toddlers hanging on the refrigerator door at home is frustrating, toddlers hanging on the refrigerator door on vacation becomes an insurance claim. While toddlers spilling juice on the couch at home is simply yet another mark on the abstract art that has become my furniture, toddlers spilling juice on the couch at the beach house becomes a lost security deposit. And…while toddlers jumping on their beds and laughing loudly and heartily at 7 AM at home is just life, on vacation it becomes a knock on the door from a disgruntled neighbor, apparently.

Last year, Jonathan and I took the kids to the beach and stayed in a small, but well-appointed condo during the off-season. It was quaint, it was cozy, and it was everything we'd hoped for and needed. We settled in quickly the first night, counted it a win when the kids both slept until 6:30-ish the next day, and carried on with our morning…on the <u>top</u> <u>floor</u> of the building. In typical form, the kids were bouncing, the kids were running, and the kids were shouting, which didn't faze us in the least. It did faze the downstairs neighbors, though. Oops.

Somewhere within the first 15 minutes or so of our first day of 'vacation', we received an angry knock at the door. Immediately, my stomach was in knots, and I felt awful. I am not a person who ever wants to be perceived as inconsiderate or irresponsible, I don't like conflict, and I tend to crumble when attacked. In all honesty, Clark and Annie being noisy that morning was simply an oversight. Had we even once stopped to consider that folks may be staying below us, certainly we would have made more attempts to keep things at a slower, quieter pace. As much as is possible with toddlers, anyway. But do you want to hear the funniest part of all of this? Feeling nervous and afraid to see who might be awaiting me on the other side of the door, I answered the knocking and instantly wanted to do nothing other than *laugh*. Why? Well, because the young neighbor who greeted me was a very-much pregnant version of myself about five years prior. I kept a straight face and did my best to smooth things over, but man-oh-man did I want to say to her, "*I am the ghost of Christmas future.*" I think she and I need to chat again this year.

When you have toddlers to consider, pack for, and bring along on the adventure, 'vacation' takes on a completely new meaning. Vacationing with toddlers is wholly different than vacationing just as adults. From the ridiculously-long list of supplies toddlers need, to the precariousness they add to hours-long car or air travel, to the impact they have on the workings of a getaway as a whole, traveling with toddlers involves more planning, preparedness for all things, and both mental and physical endurance. There's no way around it. The truth? The honest-to-goodness truth? Vacations with toddlers are *harder*. They're more tiring. They're the furthest thing from leisurely. But you know what? Every toddler vacation I've taken to this point—even those where cat herding was how I spent the majority of my days—were worth every bit of effort. Every sweat-inducing bit.

Hearing Clark and Annie squeal with delight when they lay eyes on the ocean for the first time in a long time? Watching their faces light up when their little toes make that first contact with the surf? Their look of awe when they stand in front of a certain princess' castle again? Their excited chatter during a family bike ride on the boardwalk? Hearing them refer to 'the beach house' months after returning home? It's all of this good, solid, heart-filling, spirit-renewing stuff that has Jonathan and me planning our next trip long before we've recovered from the last. We don't forget the hard stuff, believe me. Our aching bodies, our fatigued minds, and our stretched-to-the-limit wrangling skills are constant reminders. In spite of this, however, we simply hold the good stuff higher.

No matter the struggles we may face in traveling with Clark and Annie, it brings us the greatest joy to be a part of them discovering the world. For now, I'm a person my children actually want to be around. Soon enough, vacationing with lame-o Mom and Dad is going to be far less appealing. So, for as long as I'm still perceived as fun or cool or at least tolerable, I'll roll with it. Vacationing with toddlers isn't relaxing. It isn't restful or peaceful or serene. It's getting yelled at by your downstairs neighbors for being too noisy. It's sacrificing rest for yourself to push nearly 100 pounds of stroller and kid up and down a boardwalk in hopes that they nap. It's lugging a clunky toilet with you everywhere you go for potty training. It's constant sand removal and peer mediation and tantrum-taming. But you know what else it is? It's BETTER. Far, far better than pre-kid vacations. Really and truly. It's getting to see the awe of the ocean, the magic of a bicycle ride on the boards, and the tasty thrill of fresh-pulled taffy through little eyes.

Footnotes

[1] The amount of times I have gotten motion sick in the car as a result of my toddlers, actually, is astronomical. When I'm behind the wheel, it's not terrible, but as a passenger? Game over. Every time I have to turn around in my seat to help either Clark or Annie and meet their endless demands, I am instantly miserable.

[2] Oh, and you know what else you have to do now oftentimes? You have to remove all food items from your carry-on and place them in a separate bin for inspection. Normally, not a biggie. With toddlers, though? I'm basically packing a grocery store, guys.

[3] For the longest time, my favorite sugar-bribe was the lollipop. Why? Because it was a treat that LASTED. Sadly, however, Annie has outsmarted the lollipop. Her process is simple: pop it in, chomp it down, and move on.

[4] This is the point in my story at which my sister Alicia is reading and rolling her eyes at the use of the word 'awful' as far as airplane travel goes. I'll give it to her, she is the clear winner on flights with toddlers. On a return trip with a four-year-old Tristan, a three-year-old Lilly, and a nine-month-old Sydney, two of her three children became violently ill in the air. And when I say 'ill', I'm talking vomit and a pungent, continuous faucet of diarrhea.

[5] You know the one super cool thing about 5 AM runs on the beach, though? I have seen some of the most amazing sunrises that I never would have experienced if my eyes were closed. Sleep still trumps sunrises in my world, but they're a pretty beautiful tradeoff.

[6] And understandably so…their focus was on the potential for fire and not whether or not someone would be inconvenienced by their visit.

[7] End result of that one? Two chipped front teeth.

11 THE SIMULTANEOUS SAVIOR AND SOUL-SUCKER

Is it possible to treasure something deeply yet loathe it terribly at the same time? To value its benefits and yet despise its drawbacks? To understand that it both provides a lot and costs a lot? The answer—for me anyway—is a big old, resounding YES. What is it that I both love and hate equally? The screen.

The world of today is a technology-saturated world. We have smart speakers that serve as personal assistants, washers that send notifications to our phones when a load of laundry is complete, and thermostats that can be controlled from halfway around the world. We have doorbells that can be answered even when no one is home, light switches that are made obsolete by teched-up light bulbs[1], and watches that let us know when we need to take a stretch break. OK, maybe your household is slightly less wired than mine—each and every item mentioned above can very much be found under my roof...I'm married to a rather cute, tech-obsessed nerd—but take a look around you. Look at our workplaces. Look at our grocery stores. Look at our hospitals. Look at our schools. Technology is unavoidable.

From the youngest of ages, children today are exposed to and enveloped with technology. Sit yourself down in a classroom of three-year-olds and give them a smartphone. I bet you three quarters or more would be able to show you how to access the flashlight, the camera, and a game or two. In many school districts, even the youngest of students, mere kindergarteners, are given tablets to complete their schoolwork both inside and outside of the classroom. Technology is everywhere.

When it comes to toddlers, technology is super-duper polarizing. There are parents on one end of the spectrum who avoid screens like the plague and find ways to keep play device-free at all times. There are also parents on the other end of the spectrum who set no limits, or very little anyway, on the amount of technology their tots take in. And then, there are folks like me. Folks who fall somewhere in the middle. Folks whose screen allowance hangs onto a pendulum.

Some days in my home are a little heavier on the tech business than others depending on the moods of two (and often three) small-ish persons and their sometimes-more-patient-than-others, sometimes-more-energized-than-others Mommy. For as much as I don't like to rely on the screen as an 'assistant', there's no denying that it provides me with options that are otherwise nonexistent…or at least nonexistent without gobs of effort and creativity. When my kiddos are tapped into tech, they're a whole lot stiller and quieter and more contained than they are on typical terms. Because of this, screen time serves as a great window of opportunity for me to accomplish simple tasks without having to press pause every three seconds in order to apply bandages to 'boo boo's', act as a peer or sibling mediator, place one or two or three bodies into timeout, or say for approximately the 607th time of the day, "*Why do I hear screaming? Figure it out, guys! We are a team.*" Simply stated, screens keep my toddlers entertained and in one place. For the most part, at least. And…when you've got the moving-est, wiliest, most strong-willed cats on the block, these gains are kind of a big deal.

Beyond the ability to entrance, however, the screen holds yet another super power. It has the power to educate. I won't lie. My kids aren't *always* totally on board with watching videos or shows or playing games that offer academic and developmental takeaways.

Sometimes, they'd rather just veg out to something mindless and pointless and totally useless when it comes to their brainwaves. There's no denying, however, that they—and I, for that matter— have learned bucketloads of information from content that's been delivered via the screen.

In Clark's earliest days of tube-watching, lessons came predominantly in the form of life skills. Clark adored a certain little tiger, and Jonathan and I loved the simple messages Clark was given. Messages that totally applied to our toddler-heavy life[2]. Today, the information Clark absorbs is far more technical and advanced. Our guy adores machinery and electronics, and he just about jumps out of his seat when he sees that a new video has been posted by his favorite children's entertainer[3]...especially when it's an episode all about the Zamboni.

Annie's screen-delivered education has been far more academic and tangible. For her, learning came more in the way of colors and shapes, and most recently, letters. I'm one of those annoying parents (to my own children and other moms alike), who force my toddlers to sit with me, practice spelling their name, trace letters, and work on flashcards. Don't barf or roll your eyes. This isn't an everyday or even an every week thing, but from time to time it happens. Getting Clark to learn letters was a snap. I'd show him a letter once or twice, and he just got it. Working with Annie, however, was different...or so I thought.

Clark started preschool this year, which gifted me with some alone time with Annie. A few months back, I started flashcard work with my girl. It was chocolate-driven, of course, but she was all in. Only with Annie, things weren't sinking in like they did for Clark. I began my efforts with just four letters: A, B, C and D. When nothing was sticking week after week after week, I assumed she just wasn't ready to absorb this information. Thusly, I took a break and didn't push. On a recent library trip, Clark and Annie chose a cute, alphabet-themed book. We sat down as a family to read this story one evening, and away Annie went, correctly spouting off almost every single letter. I think my jaw dropped. I asked my daughter plainly, *"Annie, where did you learn your letters?"*, and her answer was simple *"On the TV."* Ha. Well, OK then.

I know that all of the tech-haters out there are cringing and developing more and more of an eye twitch with every word they read in this chapter, but bear with me. I am fully aware that for as much as screens give, they also take away. Screens most certainly take away face-to-face, human interaction and real conversation. While, yes, tossing tablets to spatting cats in the form of two and four-year-old siblings may put a temporary stop to their bickering, it's also a bit like putting a bandage on a bullet wound. It may provide immediate and much-needed silence, but it completely ignores conflict resolution and the appropriate use of words to solve problems. Short-term gains without long-term effectiveness, so it seems. Handy, yes, and something I absolutely utilize sometimes, but not a solution I should reach for often, perhaps.

What else do screens rob us of? Well, they rob us of fresh air, taking in the scenery around us, and the ability to exert energy. I myself am not a sitter and I don't deal well with stagnancy[4]. Being enslaved to a screen for long periods of time really and truly affects me. It makes me foggy. It makes me cranky. It sucks me in and aids me in easily ignoring and overlooking the people and things around me. As a writer, this is especially troublesome because guess what? Doing what I do requires sitting in front of a screen and not much else. Thankfully, my crazy life typically keeps me from solely devoting myself to writing and, therefore, it occurs in chunks. Writing is good for me, is cathartic, and gives me an outlet to reflect on and process the happenings of my life…but it's also something that can negatively drain me if I let the technology it takes to put my thoughts to paper become consuming. It's all about balance.

For the first of the Bausman children, it was a fairly slow introduction to the screen. Before you start giving me credit that I don't deserve, it wasn't because we didn't offer Clark colorful, cute TV shows when he was really young. Clark just never really had much interest in them. Always-always, he wanted to be on the move. Before Annie arrived on the scene, screen time was basically nonexistent. When Annie did make her grand appearance, however, things *had* to change. When Annie would wake to eat two or three or four times a night and then finally settle into a good chunk of sleep around 4 or 5 AM, my idea of a good time wasn't hearing Clark's cute little feet make their way down the hallway and into my bedroom at 5:30 or 6 (these were the days before our beloved "OK to Wake" clock). For as much as I loved my son, it was difficult to like him in those beyond-tired moments.

When sleep was very much needed and seemingly unattainable, something new was created on my phone: the 'Clark Folder'. Yep, that's right. My not-even-two-year-old son had his own folder on a smartphone. Go ahead, throw your stones. I. Was. So. Exhausted. When I gave Clark no other choice before the hour of about 7 AM, my tiny son would lie in bed next to me and find things to keep himself occupied in the 'Clark Folder' while I tried desperately to close my eyes for a few more moments. In those first weeks as a family of four, I sleep-listened to an alarming amount of catchy kids' songs, and I'm telling you…I think listening to that stuff in a semi-conscious state is some kind of deep form of brainwashing or hypnosis. I can't prepare or see guacamole these days without breaking into song. Look it up…or don't, if you'd like to spare yourself from my curse.

The introduction to technology for Clark may have been a slow one, but today, it is definitely a part of who we are. A small part of a much bigger picture, usually, but a part nonetheless. Nowadays, there are times when we use the screen and accept what it offers in spite of knowing what it takes. Whether it's because we've been outside in the sun for hours and need a quiet, inactive reprieve, or because someone isn't feeling well and would benefit from stillness and rest, or simply because Mommy is going to throw someone out the window if she hears another round of Sibling Smackdown commence, screens are welcome in our home as long as there are limits to their use.

With Clark, screen limits are almost-never necessary. He can take it or leave it, and he rarely puts up a fight if he's told to turn off the tech and transition to something more constructive. There are a handful of shows he really enjoys, and he does like watching an occasional movie, but honestly he's happier to play. Even when Clark does settle in for some screen time, it's not a stretch to say that he'd prefer watching a video of snow falling displayed in 4K resolution or a product review than most toddler-geared programming. Like father, like son. If he has someone to play with, however, Clark will choose going outside, riding his bike, playing with trucks in the downstairs playroom, or crafting of any sort over sitting in front of a screen ten times out of ten. Recently, Jonathan and I took Clark and Annie out on separate 'date nights'. For Clark's special evening, I suggested going to see a movie, and he was less than thrilled. He even asked if he could stay at home with his Grammy, who would be watching Annie, instead. When I thought a little harder, however, and asked if he might be up for painting pottery? Totally stoked.

Annie, on the other hand, would be quite the little tube head if we allowed it. Annie gets sucked in easily, is known for vanishing only to be found by herself playing on her tablet, and will at least consider screen time over play time. As to which she ultimately chooses, she's split 50/50 I'd say. Screen-related decisions that are a no-brainer for Clark are much more of a brain-racker for Annie. Annie's love of screens may have something to do with the fact that she, unlike Clark, was introduced to them early. Heck, we bought her tablet before she reached the age of two[5]. What I think it has more to do with, however, is the 'two's company, three's a crowd' concept. It looks like this:

Clark + Madison = almost-always successful

Annie + Madison = usually successful

Clark + Annie = occasionally successful

Clark + Annie + Madison = rarely successful

When there are three toddlers under my roof, which is about half of all weekdays, Annie tends to be on a screen more than she would be when it's just her and her brother. Although they didn't always get along as well as they do now, Clark and Madison just go together like ketchup and mustard. On an individual level, they are completely different, but together? They complement one another somehow. Clark and Madison are an inseparable little duo who have bonded hard in recent years. While Clark and Annie sometimes play nicely when it's just the two of them and Annie and Madison usually do the same, Clark *and* Annie *and* Madison just doesn't work. Not yet anyway.

Clark and Madison play together like champs. They can hide away in Clark's room for hours telling stories and arranging Legos into imaginative structures…or they can hide away in the basement for hours constructing train tracks and obstacle courses…or they can hide away in the backyard collecting bugs and running foot races. Yes, occasionally, they squabble or send my blood pressure through the roof when their adventures lead them to mischief[6], but these two jive. Annie, however, being much younger and still learning the rules of cooperative play and anything other than destruction, doesn't exactly mix well with the other two. Every once in a great while, my trio will give me a stretch or two of play that is laughter-filled and mostly conflict-free, but the majority of the time? If I instruct or insist that all three play together, it's pretty much instant screaming and tears from one of my two. Hence, Annie sees screens with a bit more regularity when Madison is around. Especially if Mommy is preoccupied with other household responsibilities. Responsibilities that can't exactly be taken care of while carrying around a toddler, that is.

Screens certainly exist around here. Under my roof, breakfast and lunch for Clark and Annie typically take place at a toddler table in the family room with the television playing. Does this go against all kinds of literature and have the potential to create bad habits like mindless eating in the future...sure. In spite of these things, however, we do what works for us. We do what we do. I've tried meals all kinds of other ways, but at the end of the day this is what works best for my family. Unless there are special circumstances to consider or events going on, we always eat dinner together without the influence of screens, but breakfast and lunch are tech-filled. Without the little bit of a tether that the screen provides me during the day when I am typically operating solo, my toddlers are here, there, and everywhere. Everywhere other than in their seat eating.

If I'm being frank, the amount of screen time I allow my children to have each day is majorly based on my mood and my current hormone level. Occasionally, even breakfast and lunch are screen-free or serve as the only tech time for Clark and Annie in a given 24-hour period. These are the "Let's Do Flashcards!" days. Other days, though? Oh man. Other days are rougher on all of us. Other days maybe Mommy's patience is on the fritz or maybe someone is feeling a little under the weather or maybe Clark and Annie are lacking the ability to get along with one another for a span of longer than 20 seconds. On these days, Mommy realizes that she can't be perfect all of the time (ha!). These are the "Who Wants Peppa?" days.

When a screen does have the potential to result in volume reduction and serve as a reliable babysitter—even if only temporarily—it's difficult not to turn to it often. The gains that technology provides, however, are incredibly finite and quite touchy, actually. As it turns out, there is a very fine line between the peace that screen time offers and the stimuli overload that it can induce. This line, as Jonathan and I have discovered, is all too easy to cross.

When either of our toddlers have been sucked into technology for too long of a period, their cat-like tendencies are heightened. They are even sassier, they are quick to snap and bat, and their attention span is further limited. Screen time, in many cases, backfires on us[7].

You may not believe it given all of the things I shared with you about my everyday life as a parent in this chapter and those previous, but I really am a halfway-decent mom. Technology is a tool that I most definitely utilize, but it's not what defines my kids or defines my parenting style or defines anything in our home for that matter…by a long shot. It's a part of who we are and what we do and how we do things, but it will never be who we are or all we are.

Far more often than we are perched in front of a screen, we are outdoors. We hike. We bike. We walk. We run. We swing. We dig in the dirt. We splash in puddles. We hunt for bugs. We coat our hands and clothing and everything other than the sidewalk in sidewalk chalk. We 'play chicken' with the honeybees and run about barefooted. I may be the mom who lets her toddlers eat meals in front of the TV, but I'm also the mom who gears her kids up in snowsuits in the middle of January when it's frigid outside and heads off to the closest playground.

Far more often than my children sit in the backseat of my car tuning me out to play games or watch videos, they are looking out their windows, starting to know their way around town, and making comments on the new homes or businesses that are being built in our community. They talk to me. They make up silly stories and laugh when I laugh at them. They sing the songs they hear on the radio oh-so-wrong and oh-so-sweetly. Don't get me wrong, they scream at me and fight with one another and indelicately throw at me a barrage of demands, too—we've already discussed the glories of car rides a handful of times—but slowly, these crazy kids of mine are learning to appreciate what a car ride can offer without a screen.

There are days when Clark and Annie are glued to the tube far longer than I'd like to admit. Yes, there are days when I might slip into the happenings of my own to-do list and realize that a solid hour or two has gone by since I've interacted with my children who are playing away on their tablets…and yes—I'll admit it publicly—there are WAY TOO MANY days when I am not fully present with my toddlers even when I am with them because of a certain little screen that just so happens to almost-always be in my pocket. Despite this, I really do think that we're doing an OK job at finding a happy medium.

Screens can certainly be detrimental and get in the way of actual, quality, face-to-face interaction, but the fact that they hold some appeal over my go, go, go toddlers has gifted our family with an experience we have only recently started to take hold of and savor: family movie night. Once weekly, Jonathan, the kids, and I settle down on either the couch or the floor with piles of sleeping bags and pillows and snacks and we relish in a bit of quiet, still time together…descriptors that don't often accompany anything related to Clark or Annie. If technology has given me nothing else, it surely has given me this. I will gladly—without complaint, without worry, and without concern for the opinions of those who don't utilize screens as I do—accept and take hold of every peaceful moment of it.

Footnotes

[1] My husband knows it, but these light bulbs drive me crazy. Yes, they're way cool, and I do love that I can walk into a room knowing that effortless illumination awaits me, but for all of the advantages these suckers give me…there are also setbacks. When they blip, it's inevitably always right at the kids' bedtime. This leaves us scrambling to restore our 'smart' bulbs to their nighttime settings. On more than one occasion, my bedroom lights have decided to go rogue when Jonathan was away for the evening. Do I text or call him for help or try to figure things out for myself? Oh, no. I'm not a lazy person, but I'm also not a person to add even one extra step in getting from Point A to Point B unless it's absolutely necessary. I believe in efficiency. On those nights, you betcha that I slept with the lights on. Problem ~~solved~~ ignored.

[2] To this day, I'm known to break into song at the influence of Daniel Tiger. I used to jokingly say that my parenting style *was* Daniel Tiger, in fact.

[3] Who is this entertainer I speak of? I'll give you three letters, and I bet you at least half of the toddler parents out there will know how to finish my thought. B-L-I…yep, that guy. He's a genius.

[4] Jonathan's grandmother's last words to me were, "Why don't you sit down, honey-girl?" I think I make people nervous or uncomfortable when they're seated and I'm not. If this has even been you, please know that I'm totally cool with you sitting. I just don't like to do it myself. This quirk of mine is a little odd given the amount of love I have for sleeping, which I would say is a very 'stagnant' activity.

[5] Actually, we bought it for the flight I spoke of in the last chapter. I guess that purchase didn't serve Jonathan and me as well as we had hoped, huh?

[6] Recent mischief: tossing stuffed animals and clothing at Clark's ceiling fan while operating at high speed and filling our riding mower's gas and oil tanks with sand. Yep, sand. Daddy was super happy about that one.

[7] Sometimes, screen time even backfires on me. Just now, I hopped over to social media to review a chat I recently had with a friend about her toddler and his relationship with the screen. Five to ten minutes into scrolling through my newsfeed, and I found myself wondering why I had even made the switch from my writing software to where I was. It took me forever to refocus and regroup myself.

12 THOUGHTS ON CREATING SIBLINGS

For those of you who had easy-going, flexible, and peaceable tots the first time around…let me just say that in a weird way, I kind of feel for you. Maybe that first babe of yours went right to sleep when you laid him or her down at night. Maybe that first babe of yours latched to your breast on the initial attempt and never looked back. Maybe that first babe of yours was always content, quick to comfort, super-laid back, and just kind of 'easy'. When the introduction to parenthood is smooth sailing from the start like this, it's obviously a win…but with that win comes one, giant, glaring drawback. And what, exactly, would this drawback be? Well, when baby number one is a piece of cake, there is a real and true potential for shock and shakeup if and when a baby number *two* arrives on scene.

Maybe a second babe won't be the type to put him or herself to sleep without a fight. Maybe a second babe won't be a champion breast feeder. Maybe a second babe will be cursed with colic or reflux. Or…maybe a second babe will just make it known that 'easy' is a thing of the past. When you're like me, however, and have a high-maintenance, strong-willed, 'you will do what I say or never know peace again' child from day one—AKA Clark—nothing really comes as a surprise.

I love my son. Love, love, LOVE my son. I love his quirks, I love his personality, and I love the way he sees the world. This being said, however, Clark is and has always been anything but 'easy'. According to his preschool teachers he is a great listener—and to that I'll just say "*WHEW!*"—but from infancy this guy has excelled in swimming upstream. Clark was a demanding enough baby who knew what, when, and how he wanted things to go, but as he approached his first birthday and toddlerhood neared, Jonathan and I knew we were <u>in for it</u>. Clark was ultra-mobile and ultra-busy and ultra-opinionated *already*, and as we discussed growing our family, there were moments of hesitation and doubt. We realized that Clark already kept us on our toes just about every second of every day, and adding an infant to the mix wasn't going to make life any less exhausting.

Considering that my children are only 20 months apart in age and Annie was anything but an accident…you may not believe it, but I really did go back and forth on having more than one. For reasons beyond my stubborn, always-in-motion son, at that. For starters, when Clark was fresh out of the womb, my body very much remembered what all was involved in growing a baby and getting it from the inside to the outside. I distinctly remembered the weeks-long nausea, the fatigue that wouldn't relent, and the Olympic event that tying my shoes became as my midsection grew rounder and rounder and rounder. On top of that, I had vivid recollections of back labor and the birth of a babe who decided that facing sideways was a much cooler way to be delivered than anything by the books despite the protests of my poor, unwitting lady parts. I wasn't exactly looking forward to repeating the process…at least, not every part of it.

And then, there was the logistical side of things to think about. The sleeping, the schedule, and the well-oiled machine that we had going for us as a family of three. With an almost-one-year-old in the picture, I was at a point of being reacquainted with a mostly-predictable life. Although I rose earlier than I had in my pre-kid days because of my 'rooster' and the demands of getting him situated for the day before heading to work, Clark had grown into a great napper and sleeper. The vast majority of the time, days at home included quiet afternoons that allowed for task accomplishment and silent nights that allowed for coveted hours of sleep. Yes, teething and illness and other variables would pop their heads into the scene from time to time, but there was routine and there was normalcy and there was SLEEP, which made each of the challenging parts of parenthood feel much less challenging.

For all of these reasons, there were days when having another child seemed unlikely. At times, thinking about starting over again riddled me with anxiety. All of the uncertainty. All of the worries and discomforts of pregnancy. All of the disruption. All of the sleep that would again be gone. It was scary.

Ultimately, however, the Annie-shaped hole in my heart and in the heart of my husband trumped those fears and doubts. The potential discomforts that a new wee one would surely bring us? Well, they just weren't threatening enough. To state it simply, Jonathan and I weren't 'done', and our family didn't feel complete. For each and every disadvantage we could think up, there were about a dozen advantages that countered it. Of course there would be long nights and hormonal breakdowns awaiting us in the delivery room, but there would also be new baby sounds and smells and snuggles. There would be more love, more fun, and more adventure. And honestly, more than we wanted any of these things for ourselves, we wanted them for Clark.

While there were fleeting moments of exhaustion that made us really analyze whether or not a multi-child household was what we wanted, Jonathan and I never felt that Clark was meant to be or was going to be an 'only'. We wanted him to live life with a teammate. We wanted him to have someone besides his parents for support and comfort and community at home. We wanted built-in play partners. We wanted travel companions. We wanted to hear laughter amongst siblings and, heck, we even wanted to hear bickering. We wanted mischief mates. We wanted partners in crime. We wanted the kind of bond that only siblings know...the kind that leads younger siblings to punch their older counterparts in the mouth and knock out wiggly, bothersome teeth in the name of love[1]. We wanted another baby inclusive of all of the hard stuff, and my body was willing to be used and stretched again. With all of these things in mind, Jonathan and I bid a temporary farewell to sleep and predictability once more, and we let the chips fall where they may[2].

For us, those chips fell quickly. Just weeks after Clark turned one and officially became a toddler, Annie made herself known in the form of two pink lines. And true to all-things-Bausman, those little lines appeared at the funniest and most ironic of times. I'm convinced that parents of infants and toddlers are on a seesaw when it comes to procreation. When they're on top, things are running as smoothly as is possible with little people in the picture, sleep is obtainable, and the cute things their children do and say far outweigh the infuriating. Because of this, they want more, they dream in pastel pinks and blues, and baby fever is real. Oh-so-quickly, however, the tables turn. Oh-so-quickly, the view from the top is no longer visible, parents find themselves on the ground, and they remember why, perhaps, reproducing yet again is not the best of ideas…which is usually about the time they discover they're already a month or two pregnant. And so, humanity carries on.

The night those two pink lines appeared…Clark didn't sleep. Or the night after that, or the night after that, or the night after that for that matter. About the second we learned he would be a big brother, Clark went from being a solid nighttime sleeper to a solid nighttime screamer. Initially, we suspected that our bud was having bad dreams or experiencing some sort of separation anxiety. Not knowing what else to do, I sent out an SOS to my experienced sisters to see if any of their babes had ever had such a sudden and stark sleep regression. They had. After nights two and three of sleeplessness, my sisters continued to encourage me that Clark was probably just going through a phase. After night four, however, I decided that despite the lack of any medical symptoms, I needed reassurance that nothing was physically ailing my poor, tired toddler. Jonathan wholly agreed, so it was off to the doctor I went. Mother of the Year over here, guys.

Clark had a double ear infection with ear drums that were near bursting. The bad news? I think I cried to know that I had overlooked something for so long that was causing such discomfort[3]. The good news? It was treatable, and within about a day, sleep returned to us all.

When we were better-rested and better-equipped to actually process the news of a second child, excitement and anticipation certainly topped our list of emotions, but there were others that were strongly felt as well. One of the predominant feelings I had early on in my pregnancy was something that really caught me off guard. It was grief. For as dumb as it might sound, I actually grieved a little when our news had time to sink in. Some of it, I think, was just that I was nervous for a change. Even when change is minimal, it causes me a feeling of unsettledness and unease, and what was headed our way was certainly no small adjustment. Life would be shaken and shifted and flipped upside-down again. Because of this, for a short time and in a small way, I grieved that I would be losing the comforts of what had come to be my new norm.

More than anything else, though, I grieved in a bigger way that Clark would no longer be my only child. A part of me hated that he would have to share my love and attention and affection before he was even two years old. Jonathan and I had always hoped to have children that would be close in age and able to go through the stages of life in tandem. Although our hopes were most definitely coming to fruition, there were parts of us that were truly sad that Clark had experienced so little time with just us. When I became a mom and laid eyes on Clark, I had never known a love so intense and so pure and so palpable. Before Annie arrived, I couldn't fathom how it would be possible for my heart to love anything else or anyone else the way it loved that little boy.

You know who helped me process those feelings of worry and uncertainty? A travel agent. Ha! Before I even told my family members that another Bausman was on the way, I confided in my travel agent (who also happens to be a friend) as she was helping me to organize a getaway. I wasn't sure if it would be necessary for her to plan ahead medically due to my pregnancy, so I shared the news in an email. Knowing that she herself was a mom to three, I included my concerns and received a lot of love and encouragement in return. Encouragement that I desperately needed. Here is what Cassie told me:

"You won't believe how big your heart gets to fit all these wonderful babies in it."

Cassie was right. So-so right. My love for Clark didn't lessen or become divided in the least when Annie arrived. When I held my baby girl in my arms for the first time, I loved her completely and totally just like I had her big brother, but the same was still very true for Clark. If anything, I think I actually loved Clark more than I had before because I got to love him in new ways. When Annie was born, I got to love Clark as my first. I got to love Clark as a big brother. I got to love Clark as my only son. And, I loved Annie equally as much but in different ways. I loved Annie as my baby. I loved Annie as my only daughter. I loved Annie as a little sister. I loved Annie as my capital L Last child[4].

There was a ton of love in my heart and in my household when Annie was first born. Love may have been swirling through the air like confetti, but the first few weeks as a family of four were certainly not all magical or—here it comes again—easy. Amongst the love was adjustment and exhaustion. There were also lots of hormonal shifts, lots of latching struggles, and lots of tears. Not so much from Annie, actually, as our girl didn't cry for more than a handful of minutes in the first few weeks of her existence, but on the parts of Clark and me? Oh yeah. We cried buckets. Those first weeks with a toddler and an infant were tough ones. They were precious too, of course, but the giant changes in our family and its makeup brought with them some serious growing pains.

Despite the reality that Clark hit Annie in the hospital the first day he met her[5]—which perhaps should have been an indication of things to come when both reached toddlerhood—this incident was isolated and fluky and Clark never had anything for Annie other than love from day one. While many little ones need time to both 'warm up' to their baby siblings and to get used to the idea that they're sticking around, Clark didn't. Annie was kind of like Clark's little pet or stuffed animal from the start. He always wanted to know where she was, he wanted to smother her with kisses, he wanted to check on her in her bassinet, and he wanted to snuggle with her. There were lots of "*Aww*'s" and endless smooches, and Annie was almost a security item for her brother. If Clark was tired or upset for any reason, it wasn't uncommon for him to curl up next to his sister, make statements like "*I just need to see Annie*", and suck his thumb on one hand as he held onto her with the other. Because of this, the growing pains we experienced weren't those in getting Clark to love or like the new baby. That part came naturally.

Clark treasured Annie from the start, but all was not well in his little world. Oh, no. Clark's life was flipped on its head. When Annie was born, Clark spent more time away from Jonathan and me than he ever had in his short life during our hospital stay. Then, when we made it home, he suddenly went from spending fun days at my sister's house with other kids near his age to being at home with just Mommy, Daddy and a baby. His ability to do much of anything was dependent upon whether or not everyone else was in a place to be able to give him attention and keep him safe. Clark was mad. Clark was ticked at Jonathan and me for changing his world so drastically without consulting him first. Good ideas are Clark's ideas, remember? And this one? Well, this one was certainly not his own.

Because Clark was understandably struggling with the sacrifices and changes involved in becoming a family of four, Jonathan and I tried our hardest to keep his life as typical as possible and to give him the attention that he both needed and craved. Thankfully[6], Annie arrived during a super-sunny, hotter-than-usual stretch of May. Clark thrives on fresh air and needs it to function at his best, so we worked hard to get out even if it meant wearing a baby or feeding a baby wherever we went. Oh-so-clearly, I can remember playing outside in the front yard one morning with Clark while Jonathan snuggled Annie on the couch, looking at my watch and noting that it was well-beyond time for a feeding, and telling my little guy that Mommy was needed inside for a while. I could almost physically see his heart break. His tears weren't the typical, whiny, toddler tears. His tears were tears of true disappointment and sadness. So what did I do? I cried along with him. Clark and I returned inside as blubbering messes, Jonathan looked at us with concern, and all I could get out was something along the lines of:

"We ruined his life. He just. Wants. To play. Outsiiiiiiiiide."

The first days and weeks of Annie found Jonathan and me learning to leave the house with two very dependent tiny persons…one of which was an unpredictable and unruly toddler who was likely to dash into traffic at any moment. And when Jonathan went back to work and left me outnumbered for the first time? Holy crud was I busy, stretched to my limit, and exhausted. When a newborn is added to the picture, the mere mechanics of keeping track of a toddler become exponentially more complicated. Tasks that are feasible with just a toddler suddenly become giant feats with a toddler *and* an infant.

Like getting a gallon of milk from a local dairy farm, for example. Before Annie: easy peasy. After Annie: physical and mental workout. The first time I attempted this on my own, I so wish I could have been an outsider overlooking my nonsense. I had a baby in a complicated, cumbersome sling which took a good five to 10 minutes to safely secure, Clark in an umbrella stroller with no storage, and exactly zero free arms to open the non-automatic door or carry the gallon of milk that I would be purchasing. Since placing a cold and heavy carton on my tiny toddler's lap wasn't an option, I somehow carried it with one or two fingers, maneuvered the stroller around the very narrow perimeter of the store, and carried Annie on my body at the same time. When we all made it back to the car alive and with milk in tow? You better believe that I took a few selfies to commemorate the occasion. By myself, that errand would have taken a measly couple of seconds. With Clark? No more than five minutes. Ten if he was being especially toddler-y. With both kiddos, though? It had to be a solid 20 minutes or more.

No matter what it was that we were doing, the introduction of a second child made life with a toddler even more demanding. When we were at the park, it was:

> **"Do I climb up this play structure carrying a baby, or do I say "Godspeed!" to Clark and hope that he doesn't break a limb?"**

When we were at the grocery store, it was:

> **"Do I sit Clark in the seat and place the whole carrier in the cart leaving me with no room for groceries, or do I sit Clark in the seat and wear Annie leaving me with limited agility and mobility for picking up groceries, or do I avoid going for groceries indefinitely and hope the skies let loose with manna once again?"**

The struggles were (and still are) real, but in having a sibling, Clark has learned so much. Early on, when Annie didn't talk back or play, Clark had to learn to share attention. He had to learn the art of delayed gratification. He had to learn how to handle things on his own or await assistance when I wasn't immediately available to help him.

Now that Annie is older, has a *lot* to say, and has an imagination, there are many more tangible benefits for Clark in having a permanent play partner. On top of this, the learning opportunities continue. Today, it's learning to share toys and snacks and prized possessions. It's learning to work together. It's learning to problem solve. It's learning to address and overcome frustration. It's learning to deal with anger in ways other than violence or volume.

Today, having two toddlers to love and care for is about finding a balance. It's about figuring out how to keep them both safe and well-provided-for, give them both attention, and—let's be real—keep them both from screaming at me or at one another all the livelong day. It's about navigating the tightrope of 'fairness'. It's about helping Annie understand why her bottom is tethered to a cart while brother's is allowed to roam free in stores and helping Clark understand why his use of inappropriate words is looked upon a little more harshly than his younger, less-aware sister's.

Having more than one toddler in the mix makes things louder and harder and crazier. It takes hands that are already full and makes them fuller. There's just no denying it. You know what else it does, though? It takes already full hearts and gives them even more room to love. Yes, my kids fight. Yes, my kids tattle on one another like it's their job. Yes, they get jealous of each other, covet their own belongings, and flaunt them in their brother or sister's face. Yes, they get physical. Yes, they have shouting matches that are loud-loud. And, most definitely yes, they push one another's buttons like none other.

All of the sibling nonsense and the not-so-nice words, though, are made obsolete by the good stuff. The stuff that makes the sun shine a little brighter. In the first days of Annie, the good stuff was Clark leaning over his sister's sleeper and saying unprompted things like *"You're so precious, Annie."* Then, as she got a bit older it was Clark offering to season her sustenance when he came at me while nursing—shaker in hand—saying, *"Want some pepper on it, Annie?"* Today, it's finding my duo snuggled up on the couch or in bed together by their own accord. It's watching them run barefoot through the backyard in the rain, giggling all the while. It's hearing the silly and ridiculous things they say to one another that bring them both to belly laughs. It's their refusal to go to bed at night without a brother and sister kiss.

Toddlerhood with one tot is tough enough. And toddler siblings? Tougher even still. Every bit of struggle, though, is ultimately worthwhile. We have our share of crazy over here and some days feel like a continuous loop of breaking up cat fights, but I can honestly say that I've never regretted adding a sibling to Clark's world nor adding her so quickly, for that matter. If you're a cat herder with another kitten on the way or a cat herder who is planning to grow the count soon, it won't come as a surprise to hear that even more chaos is headed your way. Just take that tot of yours along with your bump just about ANYwhere, and you'll hear it from the masses: *"Oh, you're going to have your hands full!"* To this, I say: *"Yep, World. We got it. Roger that, and thanks for reminding us yet again."* But you know what else I say? Bring it on! Bring on the chaos and bring on the crazy and bring on the struggle…because along with it comes so many sweeter-than-sweet encounters and opportunities for growth that wouldn't come otherwise. Savor the sibling snuggles. Laugh off the sibling messes. And reap the muscle gains that come along with all of the sibling wrestling matches you will inevitably be breaking up in a few years.

Footnotes

[1] Growing up, I was a part of an inseparable trio. I was the best of friends with my neighbors, Brittny and Morgan, who were close in age just like my two. Once, when Britt was new to the world of losing teeth and was whining incessantly in the backseat of the car over her dental misery, her younger sister solved the problem toddler-style. Morgan punched her in the mouth, popped out the tooth, covered Brittny in blood, and oddly received thanks from both her mom and her sister.

[2] Unlike countless women out there and even many readers, I'm sure, deciding to expand my family was a decision that I was able to make and carry out without obstacle. Infertility, miscarriage, and infant loss are battles that I have never personally faced. While I am super grateful for this, I also recognize that there are those for whom such a thing has

never and will never be a simple choice. For some, creating siblings may never be a possibility. If you fall into this category, I hope you know that you are seen and heard and respected by me. I am so sorry for your struggles.

[3] Yes, I am a nurse, and yes, maybe I should have put two and two together, but Clark never had a fever, was completely fine when he was upright, and never once pulled at his ears nor made any inclination that they were bothering him. Jonathan and I felt like the worst parents ever.

[4] I was never meant to be a brooder like my nutso sisters. Annie filled the voids of my heart, and let's all give that one a HALLELUJAH. In case you're keeping tabs on the niece and nephew count, though, Alicia and Joe welcomed their sixth in the midst of me writing this book. Zoey is the sweetest, tiniest, cutest little bean. I just snuggled her for the first time this morning, and it was glorious. You know what else is glorious? Being her Aunt. I get the fun stuff, and then I give her back. Kidding. Kind of.

[5] Yep. He sure did. My father-in-law brought Clark to the hospital the morning after Annie arrived, and our guy was all sorts of out-of-sorts. I honestly think he just didn't know how to handle the change in routine, the change in scenery, and all of the eyes that were locked on him and anxiously awaiting to see how he would feel about his new sister. When Clark 'held' Annie for the first time during that visit, he sort of looked around to make sure that everyone was watching, and then smacked her right across the face. True siblings from the start.

[6] And unthankfully. I'm talking temperatures in the high 80's with allllll kinds of humidity. No big deal when you're mostly stuck at home with a very-new newborn, right? Wrong. Our AC decided to conk out for good within a day or two of bringing Annie home. I'm already an emotional basket-case when I'm hormonal and sleep-deprived, but sweating through my clothing while treading my way through those long feeding sessions in the beginning? The ones where Annie wouldn't latch and I was swollen enough to give Dolly a run for her money? Let's just say that I wasn't the friendliest or most put-together version of myself.

13 A HARSH LOOK IN THE MIRROR

If you need help in the self-analysis department as an adult, there are two relationships that will test you and refine you and reveal your true self like none other: marriage and parenthood. Why? Well, because every other relationship on Planet Earth has limits, boundaries, and escape routes. Marriage and parenthood, though? Not so much. When your difficult boss or your Debbie Downer coworkers are on your last nerve...you leave them behind at the end of the day. When your own parents or siblings are driving you mad...you let the group text go unanswered for a few hours or a few days, screen your phone calls, and show up with Starbucks when you're ready to resurface. When your in-laws are one misplaced comment away from discovering your typically-unseen colors...you take a step back and ~~let~~ make your spouse do all of the talking. Even your best friend, the friend who gets you and feels you and sends you the stupidest of birthday cards that only you would laugh at...the friend who requires not even a hint of a filter? Well, even that relationship can be silenced temporarily if and when you need a break from human contact. Spouses and children, however, cannot be silenced. Or at least they can't be silenced for long. In these relationships, there's no option for escape. There's no back door or trap door or panic room or bomb shelter.

A functional marriage requires constant compromise and constant teamwork. It requires communication at all times, even when words aren't used. Marriage is deciding on a grocery list with the preferences of another's palate in line with—and sometimes even above—your own. Marriage is sticking a dagger in your cheapskate heart and spending more money on softer, 'fluffier' toilet paper even when the scratchy, see-through stuff is just fine with you. Marriage is keeping lights dimmed and turning lights off even when you prefer them bright-bright. Marriage is re-learning to fold towels when your hubby's method takes them from closet to rod more seamlessly than yours…and it's something else even harder. It's admitting that he was right. It's choosing not to go to bed as soon as the kids do even though you're completely exhausted so that you can kick back and enjoy the only opportunity for uninterrupted conversation you're privy to. It's even finding love enough in the pits of your being to save that special, hunky guy the last of this year's Christmas peanut butter cups[1].

Like marriage, parenthood requires a lot of 'constants.' It demands constant service and constant availability. Parenthood is eating only after everyone else is properly fed and satisfied. Parenthood is sleeping only after everyone else is properly tucked in and settled for the evening. Parenthood is having a moment to oneself only after—just kidding—*never.* When parenting is toddler-related, it's a nonstop hustle of meeting demands, taming tantrums, cleaning messes, mediating shouting matches, and responding to the endless calls for *"Mommy!"*

Parenting toddlers is like taking a long and hard look in a very revealing, very honest mirror. On the small scale, that mirror fills you in on lots of things you say and do without notice. Things that suddenly the little persons in your household start saying and doing themselves[2]. On a larger scale, though, that mirror sheds light on big-picture character flaws. The effort and the work that it takes to wrangle these tots and remain free from imprisonment? Well, in my world anyway, it's been slice after slice after slice of humble pie. In keeping my toddlers alive and well on a daily basis, I have learned that I'm a whole lot less of a lot of things I thought I was before I herded cats. What am I less of? How about we break it down.

I am less <u>attentive</u> than I thought.

For the most part, I'd like to think that I am an involved parent who knows what her children are up to and who is more than capable of keeping those same children safe. Even in this realm, however, I have slacked. Usually, the consequences of my less-than-undivided attention are minor. Examples? Recently, Annie took a marker to dozens of surfaces in our basement, Clark took a pair of scissors to a rocking horse's saddle[3], and all of the practice balls that Jonathan was missing for his backyard golf sessions were discovered to have been tossed over the fence and into our neighbor's yard by a certain few pairs of hands.

Once, however, my inattention was rather scarier. Shortly after her first birthday, Annie was wanting to play downstairs with Clark and Madison while dinner preparations were underway. I asked Clark and Madison if they could please help me by playing nicely with Annie while I worked upstairs for a few minutes. I securely locked the gate at the bottom of the stairs and told them that I would be back shortly to make sure everyone was OK. Quickly, I got lost in cooking. When I did stop to listen, however, and heard *nothing*, I ran down the stairs. No one was there. Panicked, I rounded the corner, noted the sliding glass door that was ajar, and lifted my eyes to the top of our play set. A play set that requires eight steps to climb and stands at least four feet off the ground. Guess who I spotted? Most definitely, it was Annie. My girl was all smiles and bouncing with the thrill of victory at her death (or at least injury)-defying feat. My heart was in my throat, I approached her with as much calm and composure as I could so as not to excite her right off of the 'rock wall' she sat inches from, and I scooped her into my arms in one piece. When I asked Clark why they were outside and how they had managed to get there, he plainly responded, *"You asked me to help, Mommy. Annie wanted to play outside, so I helped her go outside."* Touché, bud.

I am less <u>fit</u> than I thought.

I am a relatively agile person with a general level of fitness. I may not run to the degree that I used to, but I do exercise regularly and utilize it for purposes of both mental and physical wellbeing. The longer I serve in this role of Mom, however, the more I notice that I tucker more easily than I used to. We do parks and we do bikes and we do 'tag'—yes—I certainly go when I can. But at the end of the day? I am *wiped*. At the end of the day, play time on Mommy's part is at a much slower pace. At the end of the day, it's more common to see Mommy taking on the part of the 'patient' or the recipient of a haircut than it is the doctor or the hairstylist. Two nights ago, in fact, Clark wanted to play with his trash trucks just before bed. I curled up in a ball on the carpeted floor and suggested that I be the dump. He thought it was hilarious, and I call that winning.

I am less <u>mature</u> than I thought.

Sometimes, it's really-really hard to compose oneself and possess maturity when you are a parent. Unfortunately, I have laughed at far too many inappropriate things which have escaped the lips of my toddlers and instantly knew that I had myself to blame when I heard those same things 3,000 more times before dinner. Sometimes, however, I do more than laugh at my toddlers' verbal slip-ups. Sometimes I am the perpetrator myself. Like when we were playing with building bricks a few weeks back and I burst into storytelling mode. I created a scene and a story, and Clark and Annie were tuned in 100%. The main character of my tale? The crux upon which the entire storyline centered? Mister Mc-Poops-A-Lot, a lively gentleman who snacked on colorful bricks and dropped excrement in rainbow form. I probably shouldn't be allowed to be a parent. I may have been the hero of my home that evening, but trying to get either of my toddlers to look at a Lego without talking about poop for weeks after was impossible. Oops.

I am less <u>patient</u> than I thought.

When your oldest child is singing his own rendition of '*The Wheels on the Bus*' and belts out, "*The mommies on the bus go YELL, YELL, YELL...*" without hesitation, it may be an indication that his own mommy has a wee bit of a temper[4]. As a parent, a lack of patience (and all of the emotional outbursts that result from that lack of patience) is my biggest, ugliest, most glaring flaw. Yelling, at times, is what I do and how I do...and I hate it. I need you to hear me accurately on this one, too, because there have been an embarrassing amount of days when my toddlers have not only been yelled at, they've been <u>screamed</u> at. Like top-of-my-lungs, as-loud-as-it-gets, left-me-with-a-sore-throat, screamed at. While it's true that becoming a mom revealed to me just how deeply and completely I could love someone, it also very much revealed to me just how angry I could become. I will give myself some credit on this one and say that I've come a long way in the past few months, but for a period of time I felt like all I did was lose my cool.

My sister Ashley has this theory on 'half years', and it seems to hold true in our household. Her theory proposes that children function at their worst behaviorally and emotionally around their half birthdays. Maybe it has something to do with development, or growth spurts, or who knows what...but Clark always seems to take strong-willed to the next level for a solid month or two in early spring. We're just emerging from Clark's 'half year' now, and believe me when I say that I've been reading lots of materials on parenting strong-willed children in recent weeks, but last year? Well, last year was just too much for my nerves and my less-than-steadfast patience.

Last year's edition of the 'half year' found me in the midst of caring for two three-year-olds and an almost-two-year-old. It was exactly the opposite of awesome. Time and time and time again, I exceeded my breaking point, and I snapped at my poor loves. Despite the 'ick' I felt in my soul when I found myself in that place, the screaming continued to be pulled out and utilized like a concealed weapon...until I hit bottom.

One morning, I screamed louder than I ever had in my life. And you want to know the worst part? It was directly in Clark's ear. I honestly can't remember what he had done or said to set me off, but you know what I *do* know? Nothing Clark could ever do would justify such a disgusting response. My child deserved better. He deserved to be given the grace of an adult capable of recognizing that toddlers are toddlers. Irrational, still-learning, far-less-than-perfect, toddlers. Almost instantly, my screaming stopped because I saw myself acting in a way that horrified me. And then, my screaming changed to sobbing.

Growing up, I had the love of a mother who gave and gave and gave some more. She worked hard to provide for her family, she showed up at every single event my sisters and I ever participated in, and she demonstrated utter selflessness. Everything she did was for the betterment of someone else. On the other hand, however, I also grew up with the wrath of a father who took and took and took some more. Although I have come to believe in my adult life that my dad truly did love my mom, my sisters and me—even if in a dysfunctional, unreceived way—I was afraid of him, I resented him, and I was constantly avoiding the land mines of his anger.

When I screamed in my son's ear that day? I saw my dad, and it broke me. I looked into Clark's tear-filled eyes, I apologized for the way I shouted at him, and I asked him to please forgive me. I took it even further, though. In order to keep myself accountable and force myself to grow, I apologized to Madison for having to see me get so angry like that and filled in Jonathan along with my brother and sister-in-law on what had happened. I did some soul searching, I marked that date down with a big-old black dot on the calendar, and I resolved to cope better with my toddlers' nonsense. Do I still mess up? Oh yeah! But I'm telling you, guys, I've come so far.

I am less <u>authentic</u> than I thought.

Parenthood has brought out the hypocrisy in me like nothing else ever could. The things I'm super quick to preach at my children—things like...

> **"Stop yelling. We don't need to yell at one another in this family."**

> **"'Hate' isn't a nice word. We don't say 'hate' in this family."**

OR

> **"Don't grab your sister by the arm! We don't hurt each other in this family."**

...well, they are sometimes things that I'm not as quick to follow myself.

Like I said, I'm miles from the place I once was when it comes to shouting, but telling my kids not to yell at one another is still almost laughable. Especially when I'm semi-yelling it at them in the first place. And the look Clark gets on his face when he hears AND points out, of course, that Daddy said he *hated* something? It's just too much. As far as the grabbing goes? Although I'm not a spanker, I am at a times a grabber. When I want someone to listen and I'm not getting a response, I tend to grab little arms and firmly redirect them...which is especially hypocritical after sending Clark to his room for pulling on Madison's arm when she wouldn't obey his bossy commands. Oh, and how's this for honesty? Once, I actually told Clark to go to his room because I was either going to hit him or scream at him if he didn't disappear quickly. I guess filling him in on this ahead of time was a smidge better of parenting than actually doing it, right? A tiny smidge?

I am less <u>humble</u> than I thought.

Jonathan drives quite a distance to work each day and has become a huge fan of podcasts[5]. About a year and a half ago, he came home completely amped one day and told me that I just *had* to listen to one that he'd really enjoyed on the way home. Per my hubby, it had a message I needed to hear. This particular episode featured one of my all-time favorite celebrity chefs, Ina Garten, and it really and truly changed my life[6]. The first reason it impacted me so greatly is actually not the one that has landed this story in this chapter and on this page specifically. The first reason is because it led me to a belief in myself and to an attitude of boldness that, perhaps, I had something of value to say to the world in book form. Many years ago, Ina had a dream, took a risk, and leapt blindly into the unknown alongside her husband. It took lots of honing and effort, but Ina's dream grew larger and more fruitful than she'd ever imagined. I don't pretend to compare myself or my talent to Ina's, but nonetheless, she gave me permission to think big and to jump even when the landing remains uncertain. So…thanks, Ina!

The second reason, and the reason I am sharing this story here and now, is because of a perspective Ina included in this podcast that has stuck with me and relates to what I do as a mom. The concept is that of 'impress versus delight'. In her own day-to-day life, Ina has come to realize that she needs to give her efforts a purpose check before they are executed or delivered. Whether it be large-scale like the next best-selling cookbook slated to hit the shelves or something smaller-scale like the dinner she's prepared for Jeffrey, Ina takes a moment to pause and assess just *who* she is serving with her work. If her ambitions are self-centered or boastful or built to *impress*, Ina has discovered that there is only room for disappointment and dejection. If, however, those ambitions are others-focused and humble and built solely for the *delight* of someone else, there is always a sense of selfless accomplishment and true satisfaction.

Everyone likes a pat on the back. Everyone finds pleasure in their efforts being acknowledged and applauded. Parenthood, though? Parenthood has taken my me-first motives and flipped them on their head. Why? Well, because most of the time, when I put elbow grease into *any*thing for my toddlers, it goes unnoticed. Whether it's a labor-intensive recipe that only gets a lukewarm reception or a complicated-to-assemble toy that is broken within minutes of being unboxed, if I'm doing this stuff for *me*? I lose. Without Ina's perspective, it's maddening and I am left without a reward because *I* am not filled in any way. With her perspective, however, I win.

No matter what I do as a mom, the results are always more positive if I stop and ensure that whatever I'm doing is for the delight of someone else. If I'm concocting animal-shaped cookies so that I can impress a cohort of preschool moms, I'm bound to be knocked down when one of them takes a look at my efforts and points out that "...*while some moms make fancy cookies, other moms bring juice boxes*." If, however, I'm concocting animal-shaped cookies because it's a project that Clark and I can complete together, because I know he will enjoy the final product, and because I'm thinking his little friends might get a kick out of it too? It's a win even in the face of misdirected comments. And, for the record, I'm totally taking juice boxes to the end-of-term picnic. My ambition has been used up for the year, so it seems.

I am less <u>self-assured</u> than I thought.

While I will say that at the age of 32, I am finally beginning to master the art of owning what I am and who I am, becoming a parent sure did stir up a whole lot of self-doubt. In the infant stage, self-doubt came in the form of *"Am I doing this right?"* or *"Is being a mom this hard for everyone else?"* or *"Why is every other baby Clark's age already doing* _____*?"* There was a lot of newness to the parenting gig and its accompanying stresses, which plopped a bunch of struggle in my lap. As a toddler parent, though? Struggles are different.

In the toddler stage, self-doubt came to me in the form of comparison verging on competition. Suddenly, I found myself caring how put-together or un-put-together my children and I looked at preschool drop-off. Suddenly, I found myself noting that other parents were talking of sports clubs and activities that their two and three and four-year-olds were already participating in. Suddenly, I found myself tuning in to comments about screen time and organic food and what others' children were or were not allowed to do. I got sucked into feeling inferior or lesser in a lot of cases, but I'll be frank here, I also got sucked into something worse. I got sucked into feeling superior on occasion. I got sucked into puffing out my chest a little when something *I* did as a parent looked or felt good at the time.

I've been doing a lot of reflecting lately, and in the scheme of competitiveness when it comes to parents (and moms most especially), I've simply resolved to stop participating. If I do what I do for the benefit of my children instead of show…and if I look how I look on any given day because it's how I want to present myself for my own sake and not for recognition, I'm good to go. Do I still catch myself making comparisons? Naturally. But I'm so much more mindful than ever before.

I am less <u>resilient</u> than I thought.

When things don't go according to plan, I'd like to think that I'm a fairly adaptable person. When sleep doesn't go according to plan, though? Look out, World. I'm coming for you. On normal terms and with my children removed from the picture, I really am a conflict-avoiding, people-pleasing, I-sure-hope-I-don't-inconvenience-you, type of person. The tune changes slightly when my children are added back into the scene, however. And if they're added back into the scene without a nap? The tune is wholly different. Peace on Earth and Kumbaya…but wake my children, and I might kill you.

My children being awakened from their slumber is so painful to me that I have gone to extremes to prevent it. While it would be rational to assume that my gadget-loving husband is to blame for the camera doorbell we possess—the one that rings to our cell phones *only*—that purchase comes back to me. When Clark was learning the art of napping, one too many 'ding dongs' (figuratively and literally, mind you) woke my guy prematurely. Mommy wasn't having it.

If I'm being super-duper honest, sometimes I love sleep more than I love my children. Sometimes, I hold on a little too tightly to those quiet, inactive, restorative moments. Sometimes, when it's been a long-long day and I'm exhausted enough to fall onto the floor at any moment, searching high and low throughout my house for one of Annie's stuffed animals gone MIA is the very last thing I want to do. And sometimes, when Clark didn't nap and was up way later than usual the day before, seeing him exactly when he always wakes up is enough to make my heart—the one who barely remembers what sleeping in feels like—cry a little. Thankfully, these moments are finite and fleeting and I quickly remember why my children have and will always come first, but sleep is just so warm and cozy and inviting.

Being a toddler parent is hard and is extraordinarily revealing. It takes all of the effort and all of the energy and all of the service you can muster. Some days, you are rewarded with tiny glimpses of growth and a rare display of manners…but more often than not there simply is no immediate reward. When you give parenthood everything you've got and have toddlers who inevitably remain jerks on (almost every) occasion, it's a huge blow to the ego. It just is. The reality though? Tantrums are not a failure of your parenting skill nor are they a demonstration of what you are or aren't doing well as a cat herder.

Parenting the toddlers I call my own is more demanding than I ever expected. Sometimes, it requires more of me than I have to give. In giving of myself and serving others before myself and in being a part of this relationship without escape, however, I have learned and grown profoundly. Without the challenges I have faced and continue to face in being a mom, I wouldn't be standing in the place I am today. I wouldn't be as grounded. You know what parenting toddlers has taught me? It has taught me that in all actuality, I know very little and apart from myself, I control very little. So what can I do? I can control me. I can control how I react to my children, how I play with my children, how I serve my children, and how I show them love.

Parenting strong-willed, tyrannical toddlers has cast a light on the darkest parts of me, but it's also helped me to find ways to better myself. Each and every day, Clark and Annie hand me opportunities[7] to identify my areas of struggle, improve on my weaknesses, and process my feelings more constructively. Each and every day, I learn something new about my own character.

Raising my toddlers hasn't just given me the 'less thans' we discussed above…it's given me a few 'more thans' too. I am willing to sacrifice for someone more than I ever knew I was. I am willing to give to someone more than I ever knew I was. I am capable of hurting for someone more than I ever knew I was[8]. Without a doubt, I am a better person because of my toddlers. I understand more, I judge less, I embrace differences, and I respect the struggles of others more readily. My children have taught me to love without condition and to give even when receiving is very undeserved. My children have taught me to recognize my own shortcomings and to admit to and apologize for my mistakes.

Around here, there are Mommy failures on a daily basis. There are let-downs, and there are mess-ups, and there are still yelling matches. Despite my imperfections and despite however weathered or bruised my reflection may appear in the mirror of parenthood, I'm confident that somehow, more is going well than it is going poorly. My kids give me the best impromptu hugs and kisses you've ever seen. Clark frequently tells me I'm the best mommy ever. And Annie? Well, Annie cries just about every time I leave her side nowadays. All of these things continue to happen even on the days that feel all wrong. Because of this, I choose to take heart in the reality that I must be getting something right.

Footnotes

[1] My mom's sister, Darleen, makes a mean, homemade, dark-chocolate peanut butter cup. Many, many years ago, Aunt Darleen gifted every subunit of our extended family their own container of these babies for Christmas. Needless to say, we were all THRILLED. The following year, however, she arrived at our annual gathering cupless. While none of us said anything to her face about our disappointment, we decided to give our Aunt Darleen a hard time and 'surprise' her with voicemail after voicemail after voicemail expressing the great tragedy it would be to face Christmas without adequate amounts of peanut butter and chocolate. The messages were received, and there hasn't been a cupless Christmas ever since. Thank you, Aunt Darleen!

[2] Clark has a knack for exaggerating numbers just like his momma ("Wow, you gave me a gazillion French fries!") and revealed to me that I say "just yet" quite a lot. Annie, on the other hand, 'tooted' at the dinner table the other night, and when she received chastisement, you know what she gave right back? "But Daddy does!" Well played, sweets. Jonathan, do you have anything to say for yourself? Ha!

[3] You want to hear the irony that goes along with this one? Just a few months ago, we received a rocking horse from family members that had been in their possession for over 18 years. It was in pristine condition and apart from the fact that it no longer 'neighed' as it once did, it looked brand new. You know how long it lasted in my household before it was mutilated to some degree? About a week.

[4] I can't even get my personal assistant—in the form of a smart speaker—to listen to me around here. So you know what I do? I yell at 'Alexa', too.

[5] His interests are all over the map, and his top recommendations would be 'How to be Amazing, With Michael Ian Black', 'Armchair Expert' hosted by Dax Shepard, 'The RobCast' featuring Rob Bell, 'NRSNG', and NASA's 'Houston We Have a Podcast'.

[6] If you don't know much about Ina, please check her out. She's an inspiration and a dream seeker, and she is married to a guy that reminds me so much of Jonathan. As Ina's biggest supporter and fan, Jeffrey has always been the wind in her sails. For the record, I think Jonathan, Jeffrey, Ina, and I would make a super-cool dinner party.

[7] Hardly…they chuck them in my face.

[8] Isn't it crazy how much your heart can break when your child's does? This is the most ludicrous example in the world, but it demonstrates how even a petty hurt can be felt hard. Once, just after Jonathan had purchased a special lollipop for Clark, it dropped on the ground and shattered into dozens of pieces. Clark's little chin quivered and he cried very real tears…right alongside Daddy and me.

EPILOGUE: MAYBE THEY <u>DO</u> KNOW

The nature of herding *any*thing implies work. Living, breathing, moving beings have their own opinions, their own desires, and their own agendas. It's hard enough to convince myself to get out of bed, get dressed, and contribute to the world on a daily basis…and doing this for someone else? Well, some days, it's nearly impossible. In so many ways, toddlers are cats. They have sass, they are difficult to please, and their moods fluctuate like stock prices. Herding cats is labor-intensive. Herding cats is exhausting. Herding cats is my life.

Since I welcomed Clark and Annie into the world, I've been a full-time working mom, a part-time working mom, and a full-time stay at home mom. I've known what it's like to long to be by my children's side, and I've known what it's like to long to escape them. What I've come to realize in all of this, however, is one truth: Even on the WORST days, I want to be here. Right where I am. On the days when very literally all that I do is bounce from mess, to tantrum, to snot, to timeout on an endless, exhausting loop…there is nowhere else I'd rather be. At the end of the day, I want to be the one dealing with the nonsense of my toddlers. At the end of the day, I want to be the one knee-deep in their germs, waist-deep in their messes, and neck-deep in their meltdowns.

We've talked about toddler tantrums and their all-out fits of rage. We've talked about toddler talk and the ridiculous things that come out of their mouths. We've talked about toddler demands and their need for 24/7 service. And…we've talked about toddler hygiene and their lack of concern for presentability. We went deep into the pits of toddler crud and winters that seem endless. We examined the antics of toddler sleeping and the struggles of potty training. We talked 'food fights' and 'vacations' and 'saviors' in screen-form. And, we even chatted about what it's like when life with one toddler turns into life with two. After taking a long and hard look in the most honest of mirrors, we've landed right here, at the close.

Over the years, so many folks have made cute and endearing statements to me during public appearances with my toddlers. Things along the lines of *"Don't you just wish they could stay this little forever?"* or *"These are the best days of your life!"* Such little nuggets are always well-intended, but—if I'm being honest—they are *not* always well-received. Why? Well, because without fail, these feel-good messages are delivered when my children are conning the world into believing that they are well-behaved, always cute, and capable of listening to their mother. So, when a kind stranger is taken in by Annie's charm or Clark's shy grin and shares trite wisdom with me that I've heard 45 times previously in the same shopping trip, I would rather roll my eyes and let out a sigh. *"If you only knew…"*

Just last week, however, I came to a sudden realization when similar encouragement was shared with me at a much different time. My realization was this: *"Maybe they do know."* When a handyman 10 years or so my senior was doing some work at my house, he landed himself in the middle of a full, typical, as-real-as-it-gets, Bausman day. We had breakfast to prep, preschool to get ready for, a dentist appointment to make, and sunshine to be savored. We had crabby toddlers, a rushed Mommy, and anything but a shortage of emotions. There were tears, and there were shouting matches. But there was also love, and there was laughter. There was joy, and there was play. In the midst of it all and right in the center of a hallmark Annie meltdown, this gentleman and I made eye contact, I gave an exasperated shoulder shrug, and he gave me the same kind of wisdom, even in a not-so-put-together moment. *"All of this will be gone before you know it. In a few years, you're going to miss it. Even this."*

"Maybe they do know." Maybe these kind strangers—or some of them, at least—have walked the same walk, with the same, strong-willed children. Maybe they, too, have spent countless hours chasing down cats who are anything but easy to wrangle. Maybe they have known what I know now, and maybe they know something I don't. Maybe when my children are a little more grown, and need me far less, and are too big for my arms to carry…maybe I'll even miss the struggle. Maybe I'll miss the meltdowns and the messes and the misses as a mom because maybe they'll be gone before I've had a chance to say a proper *"Goodbye!"*

Already, I am at the end of toddlerhood with one of my children and am nearing the finish line with the other. Already, their hurts are getting real-er. Already, my kiddos are growing larger, and already, I am unable to comfortably carry one of them for more than a few minutes at a time. Already, my babes have realized that life has an end and that there will come a day when they and I are parted. Already.

I hope that this book has been an encouragement to all of you who live the life I live. I hope that it has given you laughter, release, and commiseration. I hope that it has validated the things you say and do on a daily basis, especially those that go unseen. I hope that my words and my honesty help us all to remember that 'perfect' parents don't exist and that while trying super hard most days is awesome and doable, waving the white flag and giving next to nothing on occasion is OK too. I hope that instead of comparing ourselves to one another or competing with one another, we can rally together on the same side of the battle against these little people who rule our lives. You can do you, and I can do me…and somehow we can both still be doing it 'right.' Let's just love our kids and do what we do for them. Let's work toward the same goal, support one another, and get where we're going even if the paths we each take look altogether different. Your kids are awesome, and so are mine. *You* are awesome, and so am I.

Every day, cat herding is exhausting and selfless...and some days, cat herding is *hard*. Flippety-flipping hard. It's giving grace when it isn't deserved, it's serving when serving isn't rewarding, and it's convincing a hostile, little being to do anything you want it to do. It's all of these things and so many more, but it's also beautiful. In the work of raising toddlers, there is beauty. In the mess of raising toddlers, there is beauty. In the snot, and in the longest and coldest of winters, and in the vacations that are everything except relaxing, there is beauty.

I can't make this stuff up, guys. I kid you not, but just the other day Annie was sitting on my lap and talking about all of the animals she loves so dearly. She looked me in the eyes, and you know what she said?

"Momma...I wish *I* could be a kitty cat."

To this, I say: *"You already are, sweetheart. You already are."*

...And just in case you're wondering. Yes. Annie is very much the sweet feline gracing the cover of this book.

WOULD YOU DO ME A SOLID?

If you enjoyed coming along on this toddler-filled ride with me (or even if you didn't), hop on over to Amazon and leave a short, honest review of *Herding Cats*. I'll love you more than I already do.

ALSO BY WHITNEY BAUSMAN

Partly Sunny: An Honest and Humorous Look at the First Weeks of Bringing Home a Newborn

> What does life with a newborn *really* look like? *Partly Sunny* is a real-life, laugh-along account of the transition to parenthood and the stark differences between expectations and realities. Childbirth hurts and babies are needy, this we know. What we may not know, however, is just how hard, how messy, and how completely unpresentable bringing home a newborn really is in the first weeks. By speaking honestly about topics like ugly thoughts, breastfeeding failures, and 'handsy' visitors, *Partly Sunny* empowers its readers to laugh at the awful parts of the newborn days so that the beautiful parts can be savored.

ABOUT THE AUTHOR

WHITNEY BAUSMAN has saved lives as a nurse, sought thrills in the form of skydiving, and burned serious calories as a triathlete. Somehow, though, these experiences pale in comparison to the exhilarating and exhausting role she finds herself in today. At present, Whitney is a full-time herder of two beautiful, hilarious, and infuriating children. She and her husband reside in Southern Pennsylvania where they savor the beauty among the chaos.

Whitney's debut publication, 'Partly Sunny', has been spotted on several of Amazon's Top 100 Lists including 'Parenting & Families Humor' and 'Parenting Infants'.

Connect with Whitney:

Facebook fb.me/whitbaus
Instagram @prtlysunnyprnt
Twitter @prtlysunnyprnt

72795501R00107

Made in the USA
Columbia, SC
01 September 2019